rather than full of resources to be consumed and exploited. We must abandon the anthropocentric worldview that has led to the Anthropocene era in which we have been living to correct the destructive ways that have led us to the current predicament. Indigenous worldviews, and their resulting approaches to living in the world, offer the only compelling path to continued human existence. For those who have worked to help protect and revitalize those traditional Indigenous cultures and worldviews, Dr. Wildcat's message comes at a critical time, as we all face the consequences of the dominant settler-based worldview that has led us to this point. Now, increasing numbers of descendants of settlers are recognizing the importance of listening to and meaningfully collaborating with Indigenous peoples as they recover and breathe life into their own place-based cultures derived over millennia of experiential learning about how to live in collaboration with the rest of life in their locales. We are living in a time where we must make room for a new, old, way to come to the forefront of how we approach our position in this world."

—Brett Lee Shelton (Oceti Sakowin Oyate-Oglala Lakota), Senior Staff Attorney, Native American Rights Fund

PRAISE FOR
On Indigenuity

"Dan Wildcat's evocative essay, . . . *On Indigenuity*, is a compelling framework to rethink the role of the western worldview in shaping our physical and cultural landscapes. These critical reflections invite deep engagement with Indigenous ways of knowing and being, to heal land and our relationships to the living world. He helps us to remember ourselves as kinfolk, in service to mutual thriving of people and planet."

—Robin Wall Kimmerer,
author of *Braiding Sweetgrass*

"In *On Indigenuity*, Daniel Wildcat makes a passionate plea for a paradigm shift to viewing the world as full of relatives instead of resources. This eco-kinship vision of the world, rooted in Indigenous wisdom and ingenuity, provides us with a powerful approach to addressing the challenges of the Anthropocene. Given the climate crisis now upon us, this book is a must-read!"

—Marika Holland, Senior Scientist,
National Center for Atmospheric Research

"Standing in the present, with an eye toward the future, in *On Indigenuity* you will travel through two time zones connected by a monumental bridge to our precolonial past. Daniel Wildcat breaks down numerous Us vs. Them dichotomies and connects all of us through becoming relatives, with stewardship responsibility for what we have in common: Earth as mother, a relationship to care for, not to use up and discard. It's a value-based, ethical blueprint for partnering with ourselves and the planet to heal and protect, guiding us through the challenges of climate change toward regenerative living, a type of living our Indigenous relatives have known for hundreds of years."

—Jerry Floersch, Professor Emeritus,
Rutgers University School of Social Work

"If you believe that, in order to confront the pending and growing global climate crisis, we need to do something differently, or even if you are merely open to that idea, you should read this book. Professor Wildcat draws from his lifetime of experience and exposure to many Indigenous cultures of this hemisphere, and many of the greatest Indigenous thinkers of our time, to carefully and clearly explain the only hopeful way out of our current predicament. Wildcat calls for Indigenuity, an application of thinking grounded in worldviews that see humankind as living in a world of relatives, in relationship,

On Indigenuity

The Speaker's Corner Books Series

SPEAKER'S
,,CORNER

Speaker's Corner Books is a series of book-length essays on important social, political, scientific, and cultural topics. Originally created in 2005, the series is inspired by Speakers' Corner in London's Hyde Park, a bastion of free speech and expression. The series is influenced by the legacy of Michel de Montaigne, who first raised the essay to an art form. The essence of the series is to promote lifelong learning, introducing the public to interesting and important topics through short essays, while highlighting the voices of contributors who have something significant and important to share with the world.

On Indigenuity

Learning the Lessons of Mother Earth

Daniel R. Wildcat

Fulcrum Publishing
Wheat Ridge, Colorado

Library of Congress Cataloging-in-Publication Data

Names: Wildcat, Daniel R., author.
Title: On indigeneity : learning the lessons of Mother Earth / Daniel Wildcat.
Other titles: Learning the lessons of Mother Earth | Speaker's corner books.
Description: Wheat Ridge, Colorado : Fulcrum Publishing, [2023]. | Series: Speaker's corner books series
Identifiers: LCCN 2023012567 (print) | LCCN 2023012568 (ebook) | ISBN 9781682753446 (paperback) | ISBN 9781682754573 (ebook)
Subjects: LCSH: Indian philosophy—North America. | Ethnoscience. | Climatic changes—Effect of human beings on. | Climate change mitigation. | BISAC: NATURE / Environmental Conservation & Protection | SOCIAL SCIENCE / Ethnic Studies / American / Native American Studies | LCGFT: Essays.
Classification: LCC E98.P5 W54 2023 (print) | LCC E98.P5 (ebook) | DDC 191.089/97—dc23/eng/20230411
LC record available at https://lccn.loc.gov/2023012567
LC ebook record available at https://lccn.loc.gov/2023012568

Printed in the United States
0 9 8 7 6 5 4 3 2 1

Cover art © 2023 Jaune Quick-To-See-Smith, used by permission
Cover design by Kateri Kramer

Unless otherwise noted, all websites cited were current
as of the initial edition of this book.

Fulcrum Publishing
3970 Youngfield Street
Wheat Ridge, Colorado 80033
(800) 992-2908 • (303) 277-1623
www.fulcrumbooks.com

Indigenuity Dedication and Acknowledgments

This book is dedicated to my granddaughter, Emma Olivia Wildcat, and all the children of Mother Earth, especially those seven generations into the future, with the understanding that the present living generations have much good work to do to co-create an environment where the world will be a more loving place for them and all life of and on this planet.

Acknowledgments must be made for those who made this extended essay possible. First, to my immediate family: my wife, Marianne (Mernie), who keeps me honest and is my best critic, and my son, Hakan, and his family, Misty, Luca, and Emma, for their love and support. Also, to my Fulcrum family: Sam Scinta, Alison Auch, Kateri Kramer, and the entire Fulcrum staff who have the patience to work with me, I am grateful for their support. They offer me a joyful relationship that few authors could ever imagine with a publisher.

A special thank you to Lance Foster, the Iowa Tribe of Kansas and Nebraska's Vice-Chair and Tribal Historic Preservation Officer, for his careful reading of my discussion of the

Ioway Tribal National Park. His suggestions and edits greatly improved my essay. Also, Dr. Bridgett Chapin, a dear friend and colleague, deserves credit for reading my discussion of her and her students' efforts to restore the damaged Haskell-Wakarusa wetlands. Her suggestions to strengthen my discussion were excellent and greatly appreciated.

For inspiration, I thank the beautiful life of Mother Earth and her ability to keep me humble and constantly mindful that the world does not revolve around humankind. Special thanks to my students, past and present, and teaching colleagues at Haskell Indian Nations University for the inspiration they give me to do my work.

Finally, I must express much love, gratitude, and respect to the giants of Indigenuity and Indigenous thinking who I have had the pleasure to work with during my life: Vine Deloria, Jr., Henrietta Mann, Bill Tall Bull, Papalii Failautisu Avegalio, Jr. (Doc Tusi), Albert White Hat, Patricia Cochran, Merv Tano, Jaune Quick-To-See-Smith, Billy Frank, Jr., Oscar Kawagley, Jr., Croslyn Smith, Suzan Shown Harjo, Bill Thomas, David Wilkins, mKalani Souza, and Ramsay Taum.

Thank you, Mom, Barbara Wildcat, and Dad, Nathaniel Wildcat, for the love and support you showed me in all my endeavors.

On Indigenuity

Introduction

Let's Get Started

Who am I writing this book for? My children and grandchildren, your children and grandchildren—our progeny, seven generations into the future.

Why do I care? For me, not caring is too lonely a space to occupy. Can you occupy that loneliness? I cannot, for I prefer to occupy love for all my relations. It is not easy, but it is easier than hate, meanness, and simply not caring . . . what exhausting work. Have you noticed how hard on the spirit it is? It's exhausting—so damaging and dissatisfying to embody such feelings. People in that space always look so tired.

Who is my intended audience? Anyone who cares, anyone who "gives a damn." I suspect there are more of you out there than some cultural commentators would have us believe. While it is an easy pose—even a hip pose in some circles—to not care, dire situations tend to make people care. Albeit sometimes for the wrong reasons, but let's not go there just yet.

I think we can do better for ourselves, our progeny, and the life systems in which we participate on the planet: what I will refer to as Mother Earth throughout this book—not as an expression of naive anthropomorphizing but instead as a statement of Indigenous Realism. So follow my words and see where they take you.

For Our Children

(A poem for all at Sacred Stone Camp composed nearly three years before the violence directed at the Standing Rock Water Protectors erupted.)

Stand down. Two words I like when directed at those whose hearts
     are filled with hate.
Stand down. A blessed command when directed at those "just
     following orders" obedient to States both real and imagined.
Stand down. Words of hope that conscience emerges amidst
     violent chaos.
Stand down. A moment—a space—where the prayers of those
     sickened by blind obedience to authority are answered.

Sit down. Just rest and think about your children.
Sit down. Leave smothering fear behind.
Sit down. And lift the cloudy veil of hatred.
Sit down. Let us visit and speak not from fear, not from
     privilege, not from authority but for understanding.

Stand up. For those whose voices are silenced.
Stand up. For those with power like plants, with roots deep in
     the earth.
Stand up. For those struggling against the systems of oppression
     that weaken our souls and forbid mirth.
Stand up. With those who fight for justice unmoved by fear and
     moved by love.

                    —Eno Etoyoc, October 27, 2013

Let's Stop Lying

Lying in most instances cannot be justified, especially when it results in harm to others or is selfishly motivated. Our Earth climate-change situation is made worse today by some who knowingly mislead the public with lies, half-truths, and by withholding the truth. Among the liars are corporations who continue to tell you they are "green" when they continue to pollute and heat up the planet. Among those spreading half-truths are those who knowingly invoke factual claims without properly contextualizing or placing those facts in our current extreme global situation.[1] And as for those who withhold facts to protect their financial interests at the expense of biodiversity and environmental and ecosystem well-being, all while perpetuating human suffering, most recognize that omission plays a fundamental role in producing logical errors and distrust. Certainly, Exxon's knowledge of climate change and the role that burning fossil fuels plays suggest that over the course of the last half century, Exxon officials used all three methods of misrepresenting the facts about how their activities have produced it.[2]

I start this essay with these difficult facts—difficult for what they say about Earth's current situation—because as difficult as honesty can be at the present moment, I see it as the most important attribute of anything we do today. The distance between those who intentionally misrepresent what they think they know, and those whose error is based on what they honestly think they know, is vast. I want to make it clear that the lying perpetrated now by people who "know better" is an important part of the climate crisis and other crises we face, but one only implicitly, not directly, addressed in this essay.

What is addressed in this book are the mistakes made by those who are honestly wrong, who misunderstand—as opposed to those who misrepresent—the world and our human place in it. Therefore, I hope the ideas offered here might cause them to rethink how they see and understand the world. Many of the problems we currently face, I believe, are associated with the dominant modern, overwhelming, Western-influenced worldview that has culminated in the age we now rightly call the Anthropocene, the age of humankind: a worldview that plays a large role in many of the global crises we now face and one not likely to produce any solutions.

As I have argued for more than a decade, we cannot successfully address the physical global climate change facing us until we have a cultural climate change. And here is the good news— there are better, more realistic ways of understanding the world in which we live. There are Peoples on the planet who see and understand the biosphere we live in very differently from those who created global climate change. Indigenous Peoples view the natural world through a lens that sees different features of the world we live in. My hope resides in the belief that a fair amount of humankind's bad behavior is an artifact of the cultural lens through which most of modern humankind understands the biosphere and our—dare I say—natural role in it.

Therefore, a different worldview, or lens, is in order. What is offered in the following essay is a worldview—an Indigenous worldview, not the Indigenous world, for there is no such thing—different in fundamental respects from the dominant view manifest throughout the modern institutions of government/politics, education, economics, and science. The worldview, the cultural lens, presented in this essay sees and understands that the diversity of Indigenous traditions resides in the nature culture nexus (NCN). A lens that sees a symbiotic nature–culture relationship as opposed to a dichotomous or dualistic tension. A worldview grounded literally and figuratively in the Earth. Think of what follows as an Earth work.

Take the ruminations, indignations, and imagination shared here and the honesty with which they are offered as an invitation to critique, disagree, correct, and improve because, after all, hasn't everyone found themselves honestly wrong many times in their life?

As with most of what I write, this is more a reporting from my experiences and the knowledge and wisdom shared with me by many persons—human and different-than-human persons. For as I have often repeated, I am rich in relatives. In fact, humanity in general has much to learn and relearn from the ecological communities in which we participate. Despite nagging fear and anxiety that rises when I get caught up in the room-full-of-mirrors world much of humankind inhabits, both subside when I step out-of-doors.

Indigenous ingenuity—Indigenuity—resides in a reengagement with, a mindfulness of, the larger-than-human community many people have forgotten, taken for granted, or romanticized. Indigenuity is an affirmation and realization that practical knowledges emerge when we take our membership in the ecological and kinship community in which we live. The deadly misstep in thinking that leads humans to think they are morally and cognitively superior to our animal and plant kin is a foreign idea to the Indigenous Peoples I have had the pleasure to meet and work with during the past four decades. Yes, we are indeed different, and it may be that our difference is precisely what requires humankind to be mindful of our relationships with the relatives, not resources, with whom we share the planet.

Given the reality of the Anthropocene, it makes sense that some of us humans need to make changes. It is not too late to address the most devastating consequences of our selfish and extractive behavior, and exercises of Indigenuity can play a large role in the remediative, restorative, and life-system enhancement work we need to accomplish, with the help of the eco-kinship communities where we live and that I hope may someday thrive, full of life.

I.

Beauty Surrounds Us

Beauty surrounds us, much ugliness, too.
Our wise ones tell us this
Both are real
But only one is true
The question is which one defines you?

There are many paths one can follow
Some are filled with light
Some are shadowed in darkness—
Even in broad daylight
Our choices matter the ancient ones say
For in this world our paths are entangled
Darkness is always at play
And survives to get in our way
To hold sway over our lives

So what can we do with the ugliness around us?
When we live in beauty
We fight with the power of truth

Never with lies
We stand with beauty
Because the Just War
Too often becomes just war.

And with that truth in mind
The ancient ones teach
In this world of time and space
We live our lives most fully
When mindful of power and place
Always remember ugliness grows
When we forget—Beauty surrounds us.

—DRW

Why Indigenous Voices Will Be the Most Important in the Twenty-First Century

In the 2013 winter issue of the *National Museum of the American Indian* magazine, American Indian Rick Potts called on humankind to take a "different approach" to life on the planet than the one we humans have developed thus far—a way of life not premised exclusively on the idea that we live in the world by altering it. In his article, "Being Human: In the Age of Humans," Potts suggests humans find a way of life where we envision "intended and purposeful consequences to our actions"—the so-called downstream effects of what we do.[3] His point is well made, but it is ironic and dare I say tone deaf that his argument is presented as if there are no Peoples, especially American Indian Peoples, on the planet that have precisely such worldviews. Potts fails to mention that until the imposition of colonial or Western settler notions of civilization onto the First Peoples—that is, Indigenous nations—of this land, many of the First Peoples by necessity had lifeways that embodied worldviews like the one he advocates.

Semantics are a part of the problem. When humans use the *we* word to talk about ourselves—humans—in the default sense of *we* meaning all of us (humankind), the use of *we* in a universal sense betrays a serious false step in understanding *our* situation.

We—all of us—did not create the environmental crises that is *ours* today. Some of our humankind bear more responsibility than others for the dark side of the Anthropocene: declining biodiversity, increased rates of species extinction, and the global climate change that, given the primarily carbon-energy source of this anthropogenic-induced global consequence, should be properly called global burning.

There are several reasons many citizens of the United States do not sense the critical climate situation we face: in our geographically mobile society it is increasingly the case that people have never lived in one place long enough to have a sense of the climatic changes Indigenous Peoples see and feel. According to the US Census American Community Survey (2007), on average US citizens will move 11.7 times in their lifetime.[4]Also, given the amount of time we now live in and move from one carbon-fueled, centrally heated, and cooled environment to another, it is understandable that we have quite literally generated what might be called the phenomenon of *insulated ignorance*. A quick Google search finds that the US Environmental Protection Agency estimates, on average, US citizens will spend only 7 percent of their lifetime outdoors.[5]

Therefore, when people say they do not see or feel climate change happening, they are simultaneously correct and speaking nonsense. Because of the way increasing numbers of us live insulated and often isolated from the biosphere in what many now call the technosphere, it is relatively easy to have no direct experience (any sense) of climate change. Hence, many people with a highly technosphere-mediated experience of the world hold opinions about this global phenomenon literally based on nonsense. It is the ways in which many in modern societies experience, speak, and think about the world that are the primary obstacles to acting responsibly and addressing the ongoing harm that extractive, profit-driven activities do to ecosystems, environments, and the different-than-human kin with whom we share the world.

No, humankind cannot save the planet. But with a little help from our different-than-human relatives, we can certainly act responsibly to minimize the destruction now underway. As I argued in my book *Red Alert! Saving the Planet with Indigenous Knowledge* most of humankind in modern societies seem determined to change everything to address global climate change (GCC), except how they live.[6] In short, few want to address the character and level of unsustainable and destructive consumption in which we are engaged. In large part this stems from the "can do" or "fix it" anthropocentrism of modernity. The problem is the myopic tunnel vision guiding what we are doing and what "it" is that we are fixing. I would venture to say there is no exaggeration in describing the modern human attitude toward the so-called natural world as *anthro*potent, *anthro*mniscient, and *anthro*present. Not surprisingly, if we believe God gave us dominion as overseers of the natural world, we have license to be godlike.

Former British foreign secretary David Owen has called this the hubris syndrome—a dysfunctional exercise of power that negatively affects mortality and morbidity worldwide. Owen argues it is a kind of mental illness deserving a neurochemical and neuroscientific approach to address. I will continue to suggest, as I have for more than a decade, that what we need is a cultural climate change if we are to successfully address the deadly physical climate change now underway.

No doubt, if their market research or an unraveling political environment shows it profitable, Big Pharma will try to produce a pill to solve this problem. Think about what that would mean for a moment, and you might imagine creative writers of dystopia, like Orwell and Huxley, simultaneously creatively elated and morally horrified with the possibilities. The real solution to the hubris syndrome starts with taking the lens of the modern Western anthropocentric worldview off and changing our prescription, so to speak, to the deeply relational people-(including different-than-human persons) and-place-centered worldviews of Indigenous People. In doing so, our desire to be remembered as good relatives, as good ancestors, replaces the hubris-driven goal to save the planet, which we cannot do, and instead recommends adoption of lifeways that promote systems of life enhancement: a good thing for us and for the planet.

In this spirit, many Indigenous Peoples of the planet have an extra-legal standing, an extra-legal sovereignty: a standing embodied in sacred covenants between them and the land, water, and life of their homelands to speak and, hopefully, be listened to, for many reasons. Ultimately, it is the honoring of these sacred covenants that secures the sovereignty Indigenous Peoples embrace.

In the extra-legal sense, here invoked, our relationship to the land is shaped not only by inalienable rights, but inalienable responsibilities to the land and the other-than-human persons with whom we share our homelands. We require no argument concerning sovereignty in the legal-rational constructions argued in US or international courts here. Nevertheless, Indigenous Peoples do find in our homelands deep spatial relationships broken and/or interrupted by a totalizing universal worldview and the Western colonialism it legitimized. What we honor and defend is a living sovereignty found in life-system relationships remembered by Peoples who continue to affirm and honor systems of life enhancement in songs, ceremonies, customs, and habits. The case made here for tribal "recognition" is one of honoring and respecting the power of life (the biosphere) that clothes our Mother Earth, and the responsibilities Peoples—Tribal Nations—have to stay in *right relations* with their homelands.

Smoothing the Ground[7]

Declarations and manifestos are difficult—for the writers and the readers. Declarations and manifestos are often taken as threatening, simple, irrational, naive, inevitable, practical, aspirational, or even absolute universal statements. All these responses suggest that for those doing the declaring there ought to be a recognition that a good number of people obviously do not understand what it is their declarations are about.

If the actions of those making the declaration or manifesto—understood by the writer(s) as an important issue—were obvious, there would be little need for that declaration. Either way, such statements are always meant to provide an opportunity for the declarers to state concisely, clearly, coherently, and, one hopes, with some degree of self-criticism, what they understand as important to those who are paying attention.

Declarations and manifestos occur based on a presumption that they will have the practical consequence of moving people toward action or at least affective or intellectual agreement in support of the declared cause or issue. Otherwise, such declarations are little more than narcissistic indulgences. Declarations are difficult, at least good ones, for all the above reasons, and I have no doubt a host of others.

Historically speaking, it is worth noting that the practice of writing so-called declarations and manifestos as explicit statements emerged with the European intellectual period of the Enlightenment. Therefore, the fact that declarations have largely been undertaken as affirmative statements of rights—for example, human, civil, workers', women's, and only recently, those of Indigenous Peoples'—is instructive. In European societies where inequalities were and remain deeply institutionalized, the secular development of natural rights and civil rights philosophies growing out of the popular seventeenth- and eighteenth-century *state of nature* arguments put forward by Hobbes, Locke, and Rousseau, seemed critical as the foundations of institutionalized inequality began to show some cracks. However, when considered through an Indigenous lens, it is interesting to note that what is conspicuously missing are statements of inalienable or unalienable responsibilities.

Even the United Nations Declaration on the Rights of Indigenous Peoples reads as a document primarily about rights.[8] In the context of where, when, and for whom this declaration was drafted, the emphasis on rights is explainable. However, I think it is interesting that responsibilities are largely implied. As I said, declarations are difficult documents for a host of reasons.

The problems that we increasingly face on the planet are the products of the colonizers', aka settlers', worldviews or, most frighteningly of all, the spirit of civilization itself: an idea that in true Hegelian fashion must reach its maturity in a world historical moment—a *telos* of universal character that Immanuel Kant and Edmund Husserl wrestled with. Indeed, this is *civilization* as a global system—the ultimate hegemonic system. For example, note the past half-century-long senseless burning of the Amazon region of South America and the attempted erasure of the Indigenous Peoples from that landscape. In the United States of America, the year 2020 seemed to be emerging as a political— that is, moral and spiritual—crucible regarding *where one stands* regarding justice. Alas, it turned out less a crucible than an endless loop of destructive behavior fueled by the information and communication technology spaces many inhabit: a manifestation of a dispiriting flat screen/flat world *eternal return*.

My reasons for suggesting Indigenous Peoples' voices will be the most important voices in the twenty-first century are many. They are based on my research, teaching, and work with Indigenous Peoples during the past thirty-seven years and the consequent firm conviction that Indigenous knowledges, wisdom, and traditional ecological knowledges provide a critically important counterpoint to the dispiriting insanity surrounding many in modern society today. As such, I am less concerned about the objectivity of what follows than the honest expression and usefulness of my observations in encouraging societal responses on a global scale to one of most serious justice issues on this Mother Earth: global climate change. I am more interested in honestly promoting justice than I am meeting conventional standards of objectivity. Hardly a radical declaration, until one examines why it—honesty—seems so elusive in the enlightened and "civilized" societies across the globe.

To prepare the ground for what follows, I offer the following statement of truths that I remain mindful of in my life.

- No one knows it all, and everyone knows some of it.
- All of what we know is incomplete.
- *It* is the cosmos, the creation, and the mystery surrounding us.
- It, the cosmos—the cosmic mystery—is less an idea than it is a sense, a feeling.

- In this world, we are surrounded by beauty and by ugliness, too.
- Never let the ugliness obscure your ability to see the beauty around you.
- The mystery is life—it is unframeable.
- One cannot create something from nothing.
- There is good work for everyone.

What follows is less a declaration than an affirmation of reasons why Indigenous voices will be the most important in the twenty-first century. Sovereignty provides the foundation for the reasons people should listen to Indigenous voices, for they affirm an extra-legal—an existential—foundation for all the follows.

hEt'A—How do you put into words experiences and activities that are yours? With great difficulty, with humility, and the understanding that Peoples of different places have an understanding of life and the cosmos that is theirs. So, take this not as *the* statement of Indigenous sovereignty but instead as one Indigenous affirmation of sovereignty: one that no doubt will appear ironic to non-Indigenous people, not for its beginning, but for its conclusion.

Indigenous sovereignty resides in the land, not as property, not as real estate, but rather in sacred natural histories where

Peoples were created, emerged, and *placed*: where they came into being, where they were given life. Unlike sovereignty as understood in legal rationales that were asserted after exercises of human power and imagined control over lands, the sovereignty Indigenous Peoples acknowledge is understood as a sacred natural covenant between a People and a Place, shaped by what some call Original Instructions received by ancestors and affirmed in ceremony, song, oral traditions, customs, and habits: ultimately, in lifeways.

Confused? Sovereignty, in the court of the colonizers, is a human construction. In our ancient Indigenous traditions, however, sovereignty resided in the land and the relationships of life found there—all life, including the land, air, and water, and extending in many Indigenous traditions to the moon, the sun, and the stars. This is not Indigenous romanticism, but Indigenous Realism. And it is the devastating reality of global climate change (GCC) that compels Indigenous actions and voices to show how we might address it as an affirmation of our sovereign rights and inalienable responsibilities.

From a practical stance, this means that in our entanglement with colonizers and their colonizing anthropocentric logic, we will continue to work in their foreign and largely artificial (unnatural) legal system to defend our Indigenous or tribal nation sovereignty. And here, one more distinction is necessary. Indigenous nation governance is not an Indian

Reorganization Act constitution. Rather our nations' ancient systems of governance are as diverse as the landscapes and seascapes, the ecosystems that informed and shaped our governance structures. For governance, too, is ultimately a natural systems lifeway in which my ancestors never saw themselves above or outside of nature. It took some of our human relatives' ideas of civilization to create that fiction.

*naw@^*—Indigenous Peoples understand that the global climate crisis is all about *our*—not mine, not yours—but our situation; not in an abstract sense, but as expressed so well in the title of the eminent electronic big beat philosopher Fat Boy Slim's song: "Right Here, Right Now." To be clear, the GCC is not Indigenous Peoples' in its genesis but in its consequences, which Indigenous Peoples are disproportionately vulnerable to, as these effects are directly experienced in their everyday lives. Indigenous Peoples experience our GCC in the palpable living ecosystems and biomes of the thin biosphere blanket that wraps our Mother Earth and in which our homelands reside.

We understand that humankind constitutes one small, albeit powerful, part of a living cosmos: a reality where wisdom and humility guide our Indigenous knowledge-holders, who constantly remind us to be attentive to our homelands and places, especially the places where we live. Our current situation, like it or not, can no longer be a *you versus me* situation. It must be a *we* situation.

Indigenuity will be exercised here by returning to our oldest tribal diplomatic traditions—for example, treaty- and agreement-making traditions amongst our own Tribal Nations, modeling nontransactional partnerships and cooperative activities based on establishing *right relations* with partners and cooperating organizations and groups.

Expect tribal embodiment of Indigenuity in the leadership and guiding roles tribes will play in partnerships and cooperative activities with government, private businesses, and nongovernmental organizations. At the Affiliated Tribes of Northwest Indians 2022 National Tribal Leaders Climate Change Summit, Don Sampson, executive director of the Confederated Tribes of the Umatilla Indian Reservation, gave numerous examples of the tribal exercise of Indigenuity. He focused on the areas of tribal policy development, partnership building, shared governance, and comanagement activities—and the humans who were creatively leading those activities and doing it, building relationships their way. With Indigenous leadership, we (it will take a concerted effort by most of us—humankind) to address destructive global climate change now underway.

naK@—Indigenous Peoples experience the global climate crisis daily as an existential threat. This threat has simultaneously produced a collective awareness that some humans are doing great harm to our Mother Earth and an individual—a personal—anxiety and sadness regarding the profound misorientation of major institutions in modern industrial and postindustrial societies. Indigenous Peoples must be heard, for they see the destructive changes in the plants, animals, land, air, and water where they live.

It is difficult for many to fathom the profound sense of loss—what Glenn Albrecht has called Solastalgia—currently experienced by Peoples of place.[9] For Peoples who have maintained longstanding ecological and kinship relations with and moral responsibilities to the life inhabiting the landscapes and seascapes that quite literally gave them their identity—what the Cherokee anthropologist Bob Thomas called Peoplehood and what the Standing Rock Sioux intellectual Vine Deloria, Jr. described as the complex system of power and place that produces our personalities—the sense of loss is palpable.[10]

This loss is too often manifested in anxiety, disorientation, and depression in their own communities and amid modern industrial and postindustrial societies. While Indigenous Peoples' worldviews and lifeways carry the solutions to some of the planet's most pressing problems, they also bear the brunt of the bad faith *collateral damage* of GCC. Indigenuity in this case will require a mindful engagement—in some cases, reengagement—with a world rapidly changing. Most importantly, Indigenuity, the process of creativity centered in the NCN will result in new practices and technologies honoring and maintaining *right relations* with their environment, the eco-kinship system, in a responsible and respectful manner. Solutions formed in a world full of kin—relatives—as opposed to resources.

Indigenous Peoples understand that the character of production and consumption that modern, advanced societies are engaged in is unsustainable and destructive. Indigenous Peoples around the world experience the downside of "progress" daily. And back to my first point, Indigenous Peoples in the face of rapid change will innovate as they have done throughout history. The injustices they experience threaten their traditional lifeways—lifeways that have little to do with the destructive environmental changes that threaten the ecosystems of our Mother Earth with collapse.

d@thl@—The misstep of modern civilization is a fostered historical amnesia—an amnesia that leads to the mistaken notion that the societies we live in, and their institutions are best "developed" through "one-size-fits-all" solutions. Indigenous Peoples know better—our Mother Earth history, natural and human, is marked by life-system diversity. Indigenous Peoples understand this: "We are all the same, we are different." Diversity is the touchstone of life on this beautiful blue-green planet.

The distinctive United States of America brand of historical amnesia is aided and abetted by the deep-seated religio-political Manifest Destiny myth. As this myth exists in the minds of its true believers, it fosters an amnesia that leads to a story of this nation that finds it nearly impossible to teach any of its democratic failures and injustices. The citizens of the United States have reason to be proud of many accomplishments, but not at the cost of ignoring or denying the continuing systemic injustices experienced by the First Peoples of this land as well as many others. This miseducative myth has resulted in a nationalistic chauvinism producing a false notion that the society we live in, and its institutions are best created by those "one-size-fits-all" solutions—solutions patterned after the American Panglossian notion that this society and its way of doing things are the best, and everyone else on the planet should follow suit.

It is time to recognize that in the push to integrate the whole world into a global capitalistic economic system, what we lose is not just the cultural diversity embodied in Peoples around the world, but the very land- and seascapes that give Indigenous Peoples their identities. Somewhere along that timeline of history, the one colonizers and settlers hold so dearly, the modern nation-builders recognized Indigenous Peoples were their—the white man's—burden, and in total ignorance—a blindness, really—they decided the differences they found in Indigenous

Peoples' cultural lifeways had no value. As John Mohawk articulated twenty-five years ago in the annual E. F. Schumacher lecture titled "How the Conquest of Indigenous Peoples Parallels the Conquest of Nature," when the utopian impulse is a worldview in which some humans are superior to others, and these "others," and the balance of the creation they did not make, are seen as resources, then the conquest of Indigenous Peoples becomes as inevitable as the conquest of nature.[11] We need to pay attention to what Indigenous Peoples around the world are telling us, acknowledging what the modern ideology of utopian progress is doing to them—and everyone else, too—if only they can step out-of-doors and think outside long enough to literally sense what is going on in the world we used to live in.

CHwahA—In the midst of incredible waste and destruction, we must listen to the voices of Indigenous Peoples because they offer hope. They still possess Original Instructions on how to live well, to live competently, and recognize by virtue of their remembered and often still-practiced lifeways that our fragile human life must be sustained and enhanced in relationships with *natural relatives*, *not* exploitative extraction of *natural resources*. It is time to move from institutions that want to manage resources to those that promote respect for relatives—the land, air, water, and plant/animal life on which our human lives depend.

Even among my Indigenous relatives who have lost so much, recollection of ancient lifeways and attention to culture in still-practiced lifeways are crucial. We have not lost the opportunity to restore, reimagine, reconstruct, and create new traditions built on ancient wisdom and knowledge. Activities of Indigenous ingenuity, or Indigenuity, draw on our recognition of the eco-kinship relations that defined our Indigenous identities (Indigeneity) and still should. The technosphere is not a system of kinship but instead an extractive production and consumption machine. The biosphere is a complex system of living kinship. It is this Indigenous eco-kinship worldview that may still help us avoid some of the most devastating consequences of the changes underway on this planet—our Mother Earth.

EshtU—Indigenous Peoples have wisdom to share about unalienable responsibilities we humans must accept to live well among natural relatives, not resources, on this planet. We also remind folks of the maternal power of the planet—this Mother Earth—and the powerful role women must play as leaders in our social institutions. In terms of establishing *right relations*, many of us have considerable rematriation activities to work on.

Robin Wall Kimmerer's book *Braiding Sweetgrass* suggests if we are mindful in our activities, we can see we are surrounded by beauty that results in a tangible sense of wonder in this world—both might serve well our hard-nosed scientific inquiries into our human lives and our relationships to the dif-ferent-than-human relatives.[12] Kimmerer's work reminds us that it really makes a difference in how we conduct our lives; she asks us to understand it as being full of gifts, as filled with gratitude and expressed in generosity.

lachU—Finally, Indigenous Peoples remind us that before we embrace sustainability, we might do well to ask what exactly we are so set on sustaining. It is time to listen to Peoples with rich intellectual and wisdom traditions that have no stories recognizable in the modern Western sense of progress—stories that instead speak of our humanity from maturity and life-enhancing perspectives of humility. How ironic that the most dangerous "myths" to life on our planet are those that promise us, human-kind, a better life and are presented as a rational material realism, and those misunderstood as romantic and unreal "fairy tales" are the stories that might actually fit what the life sciences—social, biological, evolutionary, and ecological—are telling us about the world we live in. The divide between the modern "sciences" of economics and politics that focus on resources and power as measurable quantifiable "objects" and modern life sciences and physics, which increasingly focus on relationships and processes, tells us much about what must change.

The recognition that the complex problems of the world today cannot be solved through controlled experiments, the growing recognition of complexity science, and the emergence of inter- and transdisciplinary research activities all suggest we may have reached the point where "learned" scholars, scientists, and the general public are ready to listen to Peoples who never thought in boxes or worked in disciplinary silos. We will see if those who espouse the popular apocryphal wisdom attributed to Einstein that "one cannot fix problems with the same kind of thinking that created them" are ready to listen to Peoples who know something about the world buried beneath the constantly expanding technosphere. The deep experiential, intergenerationally carried and vetted knowledge of Indigenous Peoples is exactly what is needed today. Indigenous Peoples practice a way of thinking that did not create the problem now facing the planet and, therefore, might just have some useful information regarding how we can make things better.

II.

A Time for Mending

Things change.
Yes, I know.
But change is different now.
Nature moves through cycles,
With patterns, rhythms, and seasons.
All are at odds with what we once knew.

First snow—the thirtieth of October.
A hint of winter last night and
Now another November second.
I saw a solitary junco at noon,
A harbinger of Winter
Yet, late that afternoon a pair of doves.
The small birds disappeared weeks ago.
Where? I worry.

And still the ambient light
of sunrises and sunsets
Remains so beautiful, if painted as seen,
Many would scoff at such bright colors and deep hues.
What romanticism . . .

A lone robin just appeared
        As if a prayer answered.
Look around and listen, the leaves
and the sounds they make are different now.
There is lots of mending to be done.
The biosphere blanket that covers our mother
        is torn and worn thin.

Yes, it's time to start mending our ways.

                        —DRW, November 2, 2019

Indigenuity—A Beginning

Let us start at the beginning. Before there were "Land Acknowledgements," as written pledges of recognition of the first Earth-Keepers living in North America, Indigenous Peoples of this land that is now known as the United States of America had lifeways that embodied respect for the land. Yes, they offered invocations, prayers, blessings, thanksgivings, and ceremonial traditions of gratitude. The need to acknowledge the importance of the land, air, water, and the life surrounding them came quite naturally to humans who understood themselves as a part of the natural world, who understood they lived among kinfolk—different-than-human persons—in communities inclusive of plant and animal relatives. Tribal languages, customs, habits, clan systems, social organization, and totems speak volumes about these relationships.

Unlike the progeny of the settlers and colonizers, we had no need to acknowledge and remember Peoples from whom we had stolen the land where our homes sat—it never occurred to us that it was ours to own. We were the first Earth-Keepers, who understood our homelands as gifts from the creator/creation. The world we lived in was far from perfect, but unlike the societies of modern humankind, we understood that their stories of the self-made "man" and their rugged individualism constituted their mythology. Do the settlers—the colonizers—

need "Land Acknowledgements?" Maybe, I am not sure, but we will come back to this question later. This I do know: for many of the Indigenous Peoples of North America, who we are as tribal Peoples fundamentally began with a deep, life-defining sense of place—not abstract or ephemeral, but experiential and existential. The unique configuration of the relations between the land, air, water—and for my Tsoyaha or Yuchi People, the sun—and the life found in the thin bio-sphere of this planet gave us our unique tribal cultures. Who we were, who we are as Indigenous Peoples emerged through a hundreds- and thousands-years-long nature–culture nexus: the symbiotic relationship between a People and Place.

For many of us, removal from our homelands nearly two hundred years ago through the depredations of US policy constituted a climate change event. The climate change the Tsoyaha experienced with our removal from Georgia to what is now northeastern Oklahoma, was not nearly as extreme as what the more than twenty-five Tribal Nations experienced who were removed from their homes in the northeastern US and Great Lakes region to lands in what is now eastern Kansas. Let's be clear: there was no Trail of Tears, there were Trails of Tears—dozens of them. Yes, climate change and the struggle for cultural survival is something many tribes under-stand. It is not an exaggeration to suggest that with respect to covenants and Original Instructions, the requirement to continue ancient ceremonies and traditional cultural practices was difficult.

The institutional forces of cultural assimilation laid on top of a removal from homelands was traumatic and posed the first test of Indigenuity—the application of ancient knowledge and wisdom to solve new problems. Suffice it to say, the resilience of tribes in the face of nothing less than a cultural dismemberment process is a testimony to tribal resilience and practical exercises of Indigenuity. In the face of, in many cases, already present traumas, removal to new lands required renewal of Original Instructions in principle: commitments to maintain good relations even in these new lands where Peoples found themselves. I leave it to Indigenous tribal historians to tell their stories of what this meant, but the fact that old and new "medicines" were found speaks to the foundation of Indigenuity—the ability to work with place, to find new relatives in the surrounding life—to maintain Original Instructions even in new places.

Nevertheless, the beginning of ancient practices of Indigenuity come from the deep experiential aspects of Indigenous lifeways: a sense of place—a unique cultural relatedness to a particular landscape or seascape. This awareness can be found across North America and, indeed, in many places around the world among Indigenous Peoples. Indigenuity has an ancient genealogy, for with every generation something appears in the living world that presents an opportunity, a challenge, to apply the wisdom of ancestors to address changing situations in the places Indigenous Peoples call home. And, for the last two hundred years, sometimes this has happened in places different from their ancestral homelands, given federal government policies of removal and relocation.

To my knowledge, the English word conveying Indigenous ingenuity—*Indigenuity*—has only been around since the early 2000s. The word emerged at Haskell Indian Nations University out of discussions my colleagues and students were having around 2002 or 2003. Of course, the idea of Indigenuity was presciently contained in the written works of major Indigenous thinkers a half century ago. I take no credit for the word or the idea and activities it embodies. In an existential and experiential sense, it—Indigenuity—resides in respectful kinship relationships with the world in which we live. Naturally, our Indigenous histories begin with our fundamental relationship to the land, water, and, in my Tsoyaha traditions, the sun.

Vine Deloria, Jr. famously observed in his 1973 book, *God Is Red*, "American Indians hold their lands—their places, as having the highest possible meaning and all their statements are made with that reference point in mind."[13] Deloria identified one of the distinguishing features separating Western and Indigenous thinkers as the Western idea of history unfolding in a temporal, linear sense, while American Indians think of history spatially: as a particular place and their relationship with the power residing in that place. Deloria understood that Western Peoples have seen themselves at the front of the line, leading the way, in an overwhelmingly positive progressive historical unfolding of their activities. American Indians understand their identities, as Peoples, as emergent from the symbiotic relationship between themselves and the place they consider their homeland.

The spatial understanding of a People's history and their tribal identity is a powerful idea affirmed time and time again by Indigenous thinkers. N. Scott Momaday, in his beautiful book *The Way to Rainy Mountain*, engages several kinds of narratives—a personal voice, a mythic voice, a kind of standard Western or chronological voice, and a deep spatial Indigenous voice—to tell his story. But what characterizes the Indigenous sense of that place, Rainy Mountain, is the following statement, which is the last statement Momaday makes in the book before the Epilogue:

> Once in his life a man ought to concentrate his life
> on the remembered earth, I believe he ought to give
> himself to a particular landscape in his experience
> to look at from as many angles as he can, to wonder
> about it, to dwell upon it. He ought to imagine that
> he touches it with his hands at every season and

listens to the sounds that are made upon him, he
ought to imagine the creatures there and all the
faintest motions of the wind, he ought to recollect
the glare of noon and all the colors of the dawn
and the dusk.[14]

Wise advice to all of humankind from a Kiowa thinker
and artist.

This deep experiential sense of place is the foundation
of Indigenuity. What does the word *Indigenuity* mean? At
a fundamental level, Indigenuity is about imagination and
creativity rooted in a People's deep spatial and experiential
relationship to the land, air, and water, and the life found
therein. My desire to address Indigenuity in the context of
the wisdom of humankind's relationship to the land, air,
water, sun, and living ecosystems of our Mother Earth has
incubated for nearly three decades.

The seeds were planted in a geographic information systems (GIS) meeting I attended about thirty years ago, and I
have been thinking about what I heard there, and the power
of the message conveyed, ever since. It was at an Intertribal
GIS meeting on the White Mountain Apaches' reservation in
the mountains of east-central Arizona. Imagine one of the
early GIS meetings bringing tribal People together who were
using GIS. The meeting was full of techies, and I use this

term affectionately. The GIS users were sharing all the cool things one could do with this marvelous tool.

During an afternoon panel discussion, I noticed a man in the audience attentively taking in the discussions of the technical applications of GIS. Everyone was enthusiastic about this tool and its uses. There he sat, an older man wearing his cowboy hat, Levi's jean jacket, and a western cowboy shirt. He did not look like a university scientist, but we should not stereotype what we think scientists—or anyone—look like. In any respect, when the panel finished their presentations about all the technical features of GIS the moderator asked, "Do we have any questions?" The older man stood up and said, "Yes, I have a question." I thought, *oh my goodness, was this coyote or an elder?* I expected something interesting to happen. I was not disappointed.

The man (I never got his name) said, "I've got one question. Can you gentlemen tell me about the natural law?" There was a pregnant silence, and the presenters were all looking at each other like—the natural law? Finally, the gentleman serving as the moderator said, "I'm not sure we understand the question. Could you clarify what you are asking?" Clarify your question—this was his opening. He made the following statement, as best as I can remember it: "You (the techies) have all these tools and technology, but what good is it if you forget the natural law?" He continued, "The natural law for all of us is that we must respect the land, the air, and the water. If we fail to respect the land, air, and water, we, humankind, and the balance of the life of this planet are going to pay a penalty and our lives will suffer. In the worst-case scenario, if we are too disrespectful to the land, air, and water we might even receive a death sentence." After this statement, I knew this old man was more than just old, he was an elder—a wisdom carrier.

I have thought about his succinct statement of ancient Indigenous wisdom ever since that day. Here was this elder, I doubt he had any letters—PhD, MS, JD, MD, and so on—after his name, and he got up and stated in less than a minute what ought to be the first lesson taught to schoolchildren and a reminder for every adult who has forgotten or never lever learned this existential fact. If we fail to respect the land, air, and water, we are going to suffer. I can think of no better place to start a discussion of Indigenuity.

People have talked about appropriate technologies and use of local technologies for decades. Find technologies that fit a particular environment, they have advised. How is Indigenuity different? It is different for several reasons. First—and this is a radical idea to many in Western traditions of science and learning—Indigenuity is a coproduced knowledge. It is a coproduced knowledge with our teachers, who are the plants, the animals, the land, the air, and the water. This is not hyperbole or metaphor, and it makes a tremendous difference whether you see the balance of life you share on this planet—the living beings, the relatives, those plants and animals that are of your home and homeland or the place where you currently reside—as relatives or resources.

Most—I never claim all—Indigenous Peoples of North and South America hold the eco-kinship view of the world I have mentioned: ecological in its fundamental relational/relationship- and process-based view of themselves and the physical and organismal life of the place they call home; kin-centric in the sense that what Western thinking has categorized as living resources, Indigenous Peoples understand as relatives.

The way most people in modern industrial and postindustrial societies think about technology and innovation is always going to fall short of living most fully with and respectfully of the natural LAW—land, air, and water. This is because of their resource-based view of the world. We must reframe how we think about the world, our human place in it, and the applications of technology and the designs we use and develop. Even wise-use models and theories at present are anthropocentric. The complex relational character of Indigenous worldviews offers a radical natural reframing for problem solving, something we desperately need.

Several points must be made to understand the natural reframing I am advocating. First, when one starts exploring Indigenuity, it requires the development of a keen mindfulness of the places where one lives, where one is going to build, where one is going to find materials. Our ancestors possessed technology; however, the technology they used did not require the highly processed materials, components, and manufacture that most electronic and digital technologies employ. It worked with simple materials found where they lived. Examples abound in the material cultures of tribal Peoples. Only two centuries ago it was possible to recognize different tribes by the clothing they wore and their manner of dress—no T-shirts or ball caps with your tribe's name placed on them were required.

It was a necessary simplicity that fostered Indigenuity, and genius was born from the symbiotic relationship between a People and Place. It is a knowledge few people have today. We live in a world where most people expect to make money and simply purchase what they want from corporations—corporations that are not local, that instead rely on global sourcing of materials and division of labor to produce the products we buy. And we continue to buy them because advertisers tell us we must have their products.

My Yuchi ancestors possessed an economy and technology, a know-how, based on a bio- and eco-mimicry. While our modern economy essentially focuses on the management and reallocation of resources, our tribal economies and technologies were shaped by worldviews that understood the best way to live was to understand your relationship to the land, air, water, and biology of the homeland, the place where our People lived. Because the biology, geology, and geography of the Earth are so incredibly diverse, we should recognize that the value of the earliest acts of Indigenuity resided in the impossibility of a one-size-fits-all culture.

The conditions of our existence itself forced our ancestors to think of our human engagement with the balance of that life on the land, in the air, and in the water as we developed our technology. Any other approach would have been unsustainable, and we certainly have examples of those missteps in our Indigenous past; for example, Mayan cities, Cahokia, the Hohokam complex, and Chaco Canyon, to name a few. Bigger is not necessarily better. At present, it is clear modern societies have yet to fully learn the lessons of tribal societies' experiments with civilization. It remains to be seen whether we, the First Peoples of the US, after several centuries of colonization, have forgotten those lessons.

Indigenuity suggests we should not all build and live in the same kind of houses, eat the same food, wear the same kind of clothes, and speak the same language. Indeed, it should be clearer than ever before that this promotion of that one-size-fits-all culture is completely unsustainable on this planet. We need to pay attention to our closest relatives, human and non-human, where we reside. Indigenuity is an affirmation of our resiliency in the only place it matters—the world we live in.

Although we have had an incredible five-hundred-year colonial interruption of our Indigenous histories, it is amazing how our songs, ceremonies, oral traditions, and customary practices of building, fishing, hunting, and agriculture can still teach us principles that we should apply today.

Another point complementing the emphasis on the relational character of Indigenous worldviews—those that enable Indigenous knowledges and exercises of Indigenuity—is the collective, communal, or tribal character of these knowledges. Unlike the individual creativity and genius romanticized in Western science and the arts, Indigenuity resides in a *Peoples'* experiential relationship to a landscape or seascape—not merely that of an individual person. Indigenuity and wisdom, as the title of Keith Basso's book, *Wisdom Sits in Places*, suggests, does indeed sit in places.[15] Indigenuity, as I understand and articulate it, is the expression of a collective knowledge held in—embodied in—a People's symbiotic relationship to a place: again, a landscape or seascape where the life therein is understood as kin and constitutes a community transcending merely human relationships—a community consisting of many persons beyond human persons: plant, animal, and natural different-than-human persons.

In a modern world where human activities are seen through a lens deeply tinted with the ideology of individualism, and one's accomplishments are always celebrated as individual genius, innovation, and ingenuity, it may seem odd to attribute creativity to a collective body. Conversely, Indigenous persons find it incredible that distinction and recognitions for anything other than maybe athletic excellence are typically bestowed upon individuals with little recognition for the community— teachers—from which creativity or excellence emerged. In the Western world of geniuses, it is the exception to the rule to find a person singled out for recognition or distinction who humbly acknowledges those who contributed to and shaped their work.

Performance in acting is an instructive exception. Not surprisingly, because of the explicitly relational character of most acting performances, it is common for actors to thank all who contributed to a performance or made it possible. Ruminate on why that kind of acknowledgment is largely absent in business, scientific, and many intellectual accomplishments. To borrow a quote from the popularizer of Eastern philosophies, Alan Watts, about the interrelationality of knowing and reality, especially when applied to our understanding of genius and creativity, what "we think, we know."[16]

The point I want to make with respect to traditional ecological knowledges (TEKs) is that their application in acts of Indigenuity are emergent knowledges from the symbiotic relationship of a particular place; that is, environment and ecosystem, and the People who called those places home for hundreds and, in some cases thousands, of years. Strictly speaking, acts of Indigenuity are a coproduction involving a deep, spatially defined relationship between human Peoples and the different-than-human peoples of a place they have shared for a very long time. This is a kind of the deep-space knowledge Indigenous Peoples carry. Indigenuity coproduced by humans and the plants, animals, insects, and different-than-human persons of a place is essentially a non-anthropocentric knowledge. Therefore, for this reason alone, it embodies the antidote to the destruction of the human-centered or anthropocentric knowledges that have now given us the age of the Anthropocene.

What Indigenous Peoples know and how they know might be reasonably explained in what some cognitive scientists have tried to capture in 4E cognitive theory: in short, this theory holds that knowing is more than a brain function. In 4E theory, knowledge and understanding are shaped by an extracranial environment in which cognition and knowing are shaped by relationships embedded, embodied, enacted, and extended out. Think of Indigenuity as a 4E knowledge emergent out of deep spatial relationships hundreds and thousands of years old embedded (language and symbols), embodied (customs and habits), enacted (know-how), and extended out (in our tools, organizations, and institutions).

Regardless of whether this cognitive theory is used to understand Indigenous knowledges and Indigenuity, this much is clear: the deeply relational view of the world many Indigenous Peoples carry with them produces a view of creativity that results in considerable humility on the part of those who carry knowledge; they often speak of knowledge not metaphorically but literally as gifts received from their "different-than-human" relatives. As Robin Wall Kimmerer says so eloquently in *Braiding Sweetgrass: Indigenous Wisdom, Scientific Knowledge, and the Teachings of Plants*,

> In the Western tradition there is a recognized hierarchy of beings, with, of course, the human being on top—the pinnacle of evolution, the darling of Creation—and the plants at the bottom. But in Native ways of knowing, human people are often referred to as "the younger brothers of Creation." We say that humans have the least experience with how to live and thus the most to learn—we must look to our teachers among the other species for guidance. Their wisdom is apparent in the way that they live. They teach us by example. They've been on the earth far longer than we have been and have had time to figure things out.[17]

In the dominant society, individuals exercise ingenuity. In tribal societies, Indigenuity is understood as coproduced by humankind deeply connected to the land, air, water, sun, and stars, and the life residing therein. We might consider this knowledge the result of an eco-cultural community of persons. In the case of Indigenuity, the coproduction involves plants, animals, and other living features of particular places in the world. Indigenous Peoples, as I am using the term, therefore hold experiential knowledges of places over innumerable generations. In Western scientific terms, the roots of Indigenuity are akin to longitudinal field studies of a particular community or ecosystem that far exceeds by hundreds, and in many cases thousands, of years anything modern scientists could hope for—and this is only one of the advantages of Indigenous ways of knowing.

Reliability is about the consistency of a measure, and validity is about the accuracy of a measure. With respect to the reliability of traditional ecological knowledges, the intergenerational character of the knowledge transfer contained in customs, habits, ceremony, and lifeway practices—that is, culture in the broadest sense—allows each generation to vet the 4E—embedded, embodied, enacted, and extended out—knowledge of their ancestors. Measurement (relational) consistency is ensured in the methods and practices of living cultures. This intergenerational, in situ, internal consistency testing upends the problem of internal consistency and stability because knowledges in the sense described earlier, by virtue of their eco-cultural, community-generated character, are constantly scrutinized in the context of the environment, the situation, in which the knowledge is shared. With respect to a validity test, the inquiry into methods and activities for successful living was tested every day, year-round, in the successful accomplishment of their desired goal.

As important as the reliability and validity of TEKs is, the intangible sense of belonging and kinship with the world—not of our human creation—that humans increasingly long for and desperately need may be the most important benefit TEKs offer. For those willing to undertake the work of restoring a sense of eco-cultural community all humankind once knew, and Indigenous Peoples still know or may recollect in their cultural traditions, TEKs can emerge—not overnight but over time. People must stay put in one place long enough to learn the language of the Earth and her children in that place. As we shall examine next, part of the problem with the room full of mirrors (RFM) environments—places where we are surrounded by human designs and creations—a good many of us now inhabit is that it inculcates ignorance of the ecosystems our lives—and all life—depend on. In the world of multiple crises in which we now live, the RFM effect is the most ubiquitous and unacknowledged challenge we face in addressing the destructive character of the Anthropocene.

III.

Land Back!

Land back!
Why, where . . . to whom, for what?
Returned? Restored? Received? Reimagined?
Revered. . . . Honored.

Land back!
Just politics, left of center
Right of center, front and center
No, Just Centered

Land back!
Where we began: a specific place, a deep space,
A song, a prayer, embodied mindfulness full of grace
A grounded soaring spirit found in place

Land back!
Our situation brought full circle
Through prayer, song, ceremony, and direct action
A gift entailing gratitude and generosity we must share.

Land back!
Let's talk, let's pray, let's play
Let's forget just us and find a way to justice
In the natural eco-kinship system too many have forgotten.

Land back!
A community restoration activity
The embodiment of right relations.
Land, air, and water—life-centered justice.
Land back!

—DRW

Land Back—Indigenuity in Action

Land Back!—a declaration, a philosophy, a way of life, an idea, a restorative justice principle, a policy proposal, an aesthetic principle, and more. Land Back takes many forms in the minds and lives of the Indigenous People who advocate it, a largely young generation of Indigenous activists and thinkers who are acknowledging the deep reality of our ancestors' embodied love for their homelands. Embodied love is never lost but remembered, recollected through our kinship relations with our human relatives and those different-than-human relatives with whom we shared our homelands. Embodied remembrance in our customs, languages, ceremonies, habits, songs, and oral traditions, including those precious family stories of our Peoples. In short, in our tribal cultures.

Prayers answered: young ones now sensing the wisdom that sits in places—the places that gave them, that gave us, their unique identities as Indigenous Peoples. Cultural identities emergent from the ancient symbiotic relationship between a People and a Place—landscapes and seascapes that made us who we are. Land Back, I will suggest, is a call to restore ancient covenants between the First Peoples of this land and the places that gave them their unique tribal identities: this place named by the settlers the United States of America and Canada.

At its core, Land Back offers an opportunity to begin, among other things, the necessary discussion and enactment of the cultural climate change we need to address the physical climate change some of humankind have created in our current appropriately named Anthropocene. This is an age that at present seems distinguished by its propensity for the global-scale destruction of plant and animal life and the living systems—or we might say life-system communities—in which humankind behaves so badly.

The landscapes and life systems of the Great Plains are now telling those among us who broke the Earth, the tall and short grass sod, to promote a corporatized system of cereal grain production that is an unsustainable system. Wes Jackson of The Land Institute has characterized it as a dying patient clinging to life with large doses of chemotherapy (ammonia-, carbon-, and nitrogen-based fertilizers and a host of pesticides) and an artificial life-support system (center pivot irrigation drawing on the Ogallala Aquifer). Corporate agriculture in Kansas exists as an invasive and extractive system on the land once populated by perennial grasses and tens of millions of buffalo, just as the Kansas state song memorializes: "Oh, give me a home where the buffalo roam, where the deer and the antelope play."

It has been more than twenty-five years since Frank and Deborah Popper proposed the idea of a Buffalo Commons in the *Forum for Applied Research and Public Policy*.[18] The Poppers' proposal to re-create a Buffalo Commons in the Great Plains has stirred disdain from those whose ancestors broke the sod and survived the economic boom-and-bust cycles of the Great Plains. While novelists and futurists have imagined how such a commons might come about and what it might look like, few Indigenous folks, tribes, or tribal and intertribal organizations have engaged in this restoration proposal as part of a public discussion of federal- and state-expropriated unceded tribal *lands*. Several factors explain this: First Peoples' marginalization and exoticization, survival priorities, and the existential bad faith that colonization instilled with expropriation of tribal lands, to name a few. This silence on the Buffalo Commons is about to change for many converging reasons, but central to these reasons is the issue of Land Back.

If we are to successfully address the climate change destruction we see all around us and the issue of Land Back, Indigenous voices will be among the most important this century. I say this for a host of reasons. As I argued a decade ago in *Red Alert!*, the Earth has been telling Indigenous Peoples and others paying attention that humankind will either respect the natural LAW—the land, the air, and the water—or suffer the consequences. Many now know we are paying the price for the self-absorbed, anthropocentric, primarily Western-informed worldview and the behavior it promotes with global climate change and the associated destruction it brings.

None of us should be surprised that quite predictably, and improperly, we are living in the Anthropocene. Thus far this is hardly something to celebrate with its loss of flora and fauna—our kin as many Indigenous Peoples recognize them. All of humankind should feel tremendous sadness about this loss of life, this decline in biological diversity. The overall destructive effects of the age of humankind on the land, air, and water quality of our mother's biosphere is shocking. The World Wildlife Fund's 2022 *The Living Planet Report* found an average 69 percent decline in species populations since 1970.[19]

We must remember that until very recently the biological, geological, and geographic diversity of our Mother Earth was the source of humankind's cultural diversity; we existed in the nature–culture nexus. The destruction of and decline in natural habitats for our different-than-human relatives also ensure a decline in human cultural diversity. And although this decline in both the biological and cultural diversity of the planet started with Europe's colonization activities more than five centuries ago, it greatly accelerated with the Industrial Revolution.

Indigenous Peoples have been paying attention to the world in which we live from the moment of our creation to the present. Many have stories about the cost of not paying attention to our Original Instructions: directions for how to live well in a world full of relatives as opposed to one of resources. Indigenous voices have direct experience with the deadly consequences of colonization and everything it has wrought and some useful insights about what must done if we are to regain a right relationship, as opposed to an extractive relationship, with our mother, the Earth.

What is *right relationship*? Based on what I have observed from many elders—not old people but people with a deep mindfulness, an awareness and attentiveness to their tribal traditions and the places they call home—right relationship assumes a position of humility about power and knowing and therefore encourages mindfulness regarding our activities and behavior. Right relationships express a humility based on a non-anthropocentric worldview. In fact, my experience with Indigenous wisdom-keepers suggests the notion that the world revolves around humans is foreign to most of Indigenous worldviews and may be the most dangerous misstep modern humankind has taken.

Therefore, creating a place, an environment, of *right relations* entails responsible and respectful relations with our community in the fullest sense: a community made up of human persons and different-than-human natural plant and animal persons and features of the natural world, all constituting a system of kinship richer and more complex than a merely human community of persons. The first separation we must challenge is the way in which modern humans have shaped a worldview that has segregated many of our relatives into a realm of resources.

It makes a tremendous difference in one's conduct if one sees the world as full of resources or as inhabited by relatives. The world of humans and resources results in an anthropocentric worldview that inevitably leads us to spend a tremendous amount of time arguing about who has the right to use this or that resource, whereas the world inhabited by relatives shifts our focus to questions of respect and responsibilities. The *right relations* I speak of necessarily involve a serious examination of how we live in relationship to the plants, animals, and different-than-human persons—our natural relatives—that make up our eco-cultural communities—communities that form a distinct personality or identity emergent from the symbiotic relationship of people and place. In short, an expression of *right relations* extends beyond mere consideration of relationships to other humans. *Right relations* take us back to the natural LAW of the land, air, and water on which the biology of the planet depends.

Indigenous voices will be the most important voices because, as I've noted, it is impossible to solve problems with the same kind of thinking that created them, and we need to listen to Peoples whose thinking does not conform to the universalizing Western worldview. Indigenous Peoples came by their knowledges by developing a keen awareness, an attentiveness, a mindfulness, of the world around them. We may indeed look at the world through a human lens. But knowing this and understanding that the life around us also senses the world in ways that we cannot provides an opportunity to seek a correction, with their assistance, experientially through mindful attentiveness, ceremony, dreams, visions of the world we live in, and exercises of Indigenuity.

My friend and mentor Vine Deloria, Jr. spoke of and wrote a book about "the world we used to live in."[20] Read it carefully front to back and you will see how Deloria ultimately suggests that the world—the one we used to live in—is still there. The fact that modern civilized humankind cannot see it is a statement about what a great many of us have lost and what only a few still see, experience, and can understand. We must reengage the ancient kinship way of knowing that allowed us to see and understand the world through a fundamentally relational, or ecological and kinship lens.

Modern, technologically savvy humankind has certainly tried to shape the world to fit us with the one-size-fits-all culture, but the good news is we have not changed it so much that the Earth's wisdom and power have disappeared. Those willing to step outside their self, their ego and ambitions, will be surprised by what they find. As Robin Kimmerer tells us in her gift to us, *Braiding Sweetgrass*, the natural world is very much a spiritual world, rich in gifts, waiting to be shared with those of our humankind willing to watch, listen, breathe, touch, and taste rather than dissecting and reducing living things to parts.

An excellent example of Land Back can be found in the Iowa Tribe of Kansas and Nebraska's creation of their Ioway Tribal National Park. Their story in broad outline is all too familiar for the few who know the untold history of the dozens of Trails of Tears stories that occurred in the nineteenth century. Most children learn *the* Trail of Tears story of the removal of the so-called Five Civilized Tribes of the southeastern United States, and that is a problem. They think that was it—the Trail of Tears of the Choctaw, Chickasaw, Cherokee, Muscogee, and Seminole to Indian Territory in what is now known as Oklahoma. And that is an example of the miseducative narrative of US history that continues to dominate most US history books.

There were actually dozens of Trails of Tears stories: tribes from as far east as New York State and between the Ohio River and the Great Lakes were moved west between 1830 and 1850. More than twenty tribes ended up in eastern Kansas Territory by 1854. The story shared by the eastern and Great Lakes tribes removed to Kansas goes something like this: encroachment of tribal homelands, disease/pandemics, war, cultural assimilation, and nineteenth-century depredations inflicted by federal Indian policies that removed them from ancestral lands to small reservations, reducing their land base. By the time Kansas became a state, many of these "relocated" tribes faced drastic changes and an even more dire struggle for continued tribal existence.

Four of the emigrant, or relocated, tribes: Iowa, Kickapoo, Potawatomi, and the Sac and Fox tribes had their reservations established on land in what is now northeast Kansas. Each tribe has its own modern history, but the current activities of the small Iowa Tribe of Kansas and Nebraska deserve mention, for they represent a compelling example of Land Back as an exercise of Indigenuity.

The Ioway Tribal National Park

In 2018 and 2020 The Nature Conservancy reached agreements to return 444 acres of ancestral tribal lands to the Iowa, then known as the Rulo Bluff Preserve. In the midst of the Land Back activity, the Missouri River flood of 2019 and the COVID-19 pandemic in 2020 presented the Ioway (they call themselves Boxaje) with challenges for their tribal economy and land management program. Iowa (Ioway) Tribe of Kansas and Nebraska's vice-chair and tribal historic preservation officer, Lance Foster, wondered whether the Ioway could create a tribal national park to help address the many challenges they were facing.

Foster found that the Red Cliff Band of Lake Superior Chippewa tribal nation created the first exclusively tribally governed and managed national park in the US in 2017: Frog Bay National Park. Determined to pursue a tribal national park for the Iowa (Ioway) tribe, Foster presented the idea to the tribal council. On June 17, 2020, the Iowa tribal council passed a resolution to create the Ioway Tribal National Park, or in their language, Baxoje Mowotanani, meaning the Ioway land of original condition, providing wild plant foods and medicines. The tribal leadership decided to take the returned Rulo Bluffs area, along with 120 acres they owned—known as the Leary parcel, site of an ancestral village from the 1200s to the 1400s and designated a National Historic Landmark in 1964—to create the largest tribal national park in the United States. As of 2023, the

Ioway have added small parcels—a tribal tract of land known as Dupuis Hollow and a parcel of land owned by the state of Kansas where a Presbyterian mission was built in 1844—bringing Baxoje Mowotanani's total acreage to 811. Currently, the tribe is evaluating additional sites for protection.

In another exercise of land-related Indigenuity, the Iowa (Ioway) Tribe of Kansas and Nebraska was the first Indigenous nation in the US to establish, on a nation-to-nation bilateral agreement, a sister park relationship between their tribal national park and the National Park Service–managed Effigy Mounds National Monument in the state of Iowa.[21] After years of mismanagement and acts of desecration, the Iowa Tribe is trying to forge a new relationship of mutual respect, cooperation, and accountability with the US National Park Service.

Although I will focus on their tribal national park initiative, it should be noted that the Iowa Tribe's regenerative agricultural efforts—for example, non-GMO soybean and hemp farming—are part of an overall plan for the Iowa to return to regenerative lifeway relationships in the place they call home. In short, they decided to address the present-day problems they were facing on their small reservation by applying the ancient wisdom of the ancestors—to exercise what I call Indigenuity in a tribal Land Back activity.

Landback.org has done an incredible job of trying to educate the world about Land Back. Their website offers a good description of Land Back and organizing principles for their work. Much that follows resonates with the ideas Landback.org advocates. My own work has led me to think of Land Back as involving three basic principles. First, it is about putting our human selves in *right relations* with the natural LAW: the land, air, water and the plants and animals with whom we share the land. Second, Land Back embraces an understanding of the NCN. Finally, and logically following the first two principles, it embraces a non-anthropocentric worldview. The activities of the Iowa Tribe of Kansas and Nebraska over the last decade offer one example of what Land Back might embody for a tribal nation. Other tribal examples are bound to follow in the next decade across the United States and around the world.

Right Relations

When most Americans think of the US government's system of national parks, most of which are part of ill-gotten gains facilitated by a plenary power that Congress exercises over so-called Indian Affairs, they think of an escape or a retreat to a natural place where they can recreate and enjoy "nature." When Indigenous Peoples like the Iowa of Kansas and Nebraska and the Red Cliff Band of Lake Superior Chippewa decided to establish their national parks, the activity is better described as a reintegration and restoration of ancient eco-cultural kinship systems they were part of before the European and

Euro-American settlers invaded their homelands. As Lance Foster, Iowa Tribe historic preservation officer, succinctly states in a *National Parks Traveler* podcast in 2021, their park would be a place of "perpetuation, preservation, and conservation for future generations and for the species there."

In discussing the genesis of the tribal national park idea, Foster said,

> I just saw the beauty of the trees. The beauty of the birds and, I guess, I felt sad so much was taken away and so much in pain compared to what I was used to. And then getting to know people, to see how we had to survive, how we had to transform ourselves to survive. So much had been lost: so much of our language, so much of our traditions, and stuff that I thought, you know, as one of my Cheyenne uncles, Herman Bears Come Out, told me, "If it was ever out there, it still is out there and that is where you need to find it."[22]

Foster speaks about the importance of preserving small pieces of land that embody "Mowotananyi"—the original land. He explains the original land is the way the creator made it, and while "these are just little tiny pieces, like .001 of what was there," they must be protected. As he states, it is to "help our people kind of find themselves and reconnect themselves through the land." The Iowa efforts embody *right relations* as responsible, restorative, and regenerative activities. There is no rational monetary calculation of what they can extract from the land or how they can profit from it. Instead, there is an affirmation that minus *right relations*, what it means to be Iowa becomes very difficult.

The Nature–Culture Nexus

Listening to Foster speak about the Iowa Tribe's national park and the tribe's regenerative agriculture activities, one can sense that all these activities are of the same "cloth." John Mohawk, Onondaga philosopher, often emphasized that the complex web of life that modernity unraveled, tore, and frayed must be mended if we expect to live well. This mending involves an active affirmation of the nature–culture nexus. Restoring the symbiotic relationship between a People and a Place is crucial today, and the Iowa Tribe's national park is actively engaged in this work. Foster makes it clear that their first concern is to provide a place for the NCN to thrive for their Iowa People. As their three-centuries-long struggle with colonialism indicates, the Iowa NCN became frayed and torn with the loss many of the places they once called home. Now they have summer internship programs that get their youth out on the land again. Language, culture, and natural sciences are taught, and a sense of wellness and pride in who the Iowa is being restored.

While Foster says the primary reason for the park's establishment is their Iowa People, he also feels the park will help others who have a sense that something is missing in their lives feel a connection to natural places. What strikes one is how sensitive Foster is to what has been lost and his recognition that there are many on the planet who recognize a similar loss. Here again, one is struck by the big picture of Foster's thinking. He envisions programs in the park and the historic Great Nemaha River Trading Post, also owned by the tribe, that will share their history and culture with non-Iowa people. The power of place that drew Foster home and the sharing of the Iowas' resiliency may inspire others to think about putting themselves in *right relations* with First Peoples and the land where they now reside.

Although humankind has greatly disturbed—and in many cases damaged—the land and her first caretakers, the activities of the Iowa Tribe provide an example of what Land Back can look like if we go about mindfully restoring the NCN. In so doing, we may begin to heal the damage humankind has done to Mother Earth and her Peoples—the human and different-than-human. Our insulation and separation from the life that surrounds us is the problem. If one frames Land Back at its core as the restoration of the vibrant nature–culture nexus that once gave all humankind its unique cultural character, there is reason for hope. There is much we can still learn from the land, air, water, and the life with whom we share this planet.

A Non-Anthropocentric Worldview

Kirkpatrick Sale, in his classic work *The Conquest of Paradise*, argues the modern Western worldview was present in the fifteenth-century Europe.[23] Humanism, rationalism, and materialism were well-formed ideologies, Sale contends, that shaped the collision of worldviews that continues today. Indigenous North American worldviews, like many around the world, would find the humanism, where man is the measure of all things, ludicrous. Land Back as conceptualized here understands it as going back to the land to listen, learn, and leave behind the anthropocentric thinking that has quite predictably given us the age of the Anthropocene along with the current anthropogenic loss of biodiversity, natural habitats, and species—as well as a host of destructive extreme weather events caused by global climate change.

Henry Bears Come Out's insight, shared with Mr. Foster, that "if it was ever out there, it still is out there and that is where you need to find it," is a statement that acknowledges the world is hardly all about us. Rather, the knowledge of who we are, what we know, and the beauty of the world is still out there. The Iowa National Park embodies the ancient Indigenous wisdom that we—humankind—need a lot of help from teachers who are older than humankind and have much to share, if we just start paying attention. The Iowa National Park is a Land Acknowledgement, a model of Land Back, an act of Indigenuity, and a blessing. We should all be thankful that there are increasing numbers of Tribal Nations undertaking their own Land Back actions.

Fifty years ago, Vine Deloria, Jr. ended his *landmark* book, *God Is Red*, with several questions and two predictions:

> Who will find peace with the lands? The future of humankind lies waiting for those who will come to understand their lives and take up their responsibilities to all living things. Who will listen to the trees, the animals and birds, the voices of the places of the land? As the long-forgotten peoples of the respective continents rise and begin to reclaim their ancient heritage, they will discover the meaning of the lands of their ancestors. That is when the invaders of the North American continent will finally discover that for this land, God is red.[24]

The Iowa Tribe of Kansas and Nebraska has answered both questions. As for his predictions? The Iowa are certainly discovering "the meaning of the lands of their ancestors." And as for the invaders of the North American continent, it remains to be seen if they have discovered "that for this land, God is red."

IV.

To See in a Different Light

To see in a different light always fascinated me
I remember as a young child seeing things
I had never seen before—because of the light
Ambient light from an overcast sky
Or a diffused light at dusk through the autumn leaves
You know or do you?
How the world—everything that I could see of it—
With sunlight, moonlight, and starlight streaming in a room
Even gave the room a character of beauty
I had never seen before
How looking out my bedroom window once
I saw things from a far distance, a hillside
I had never seen before
It was either late autumn or late winter
I wondered why I had not seen the hillside before
At the time I attributed the sight of the beautiful hillside
To the season and the light
And I was right the bare trees revealed a beauty
I could not see through their leaves until then

But the trees disrobed revealed a sight
I had never seen before
I could see in a different light.

—DRW

Indigenuity, the Waste Problem, and a Wetlands Example

We have a waste problem on the land, in the air, and in the water. On the land, we in the US put 140 million tons of waste a year in landfills (some suggest as much of 50 percent, the EPA says 43 percent, that could have been recycled). Do the math. On average a person (infants included) living in the US produces approximately 855 pounds of landfill waste a year, and that is just the beginning of a *mis*consumption story one finds when we dig into our trash. By misconsumption, I mean we buy a lot of advertising, packaging, and products we do not need. We consume badly for ourselves and the planet, and the result is waste.

In the air, excluding the twenty-three thousand pieces of space junk orbiting the Earth that technically are not a part of the biosphere—unless they return to Earth—our waste problem is largely the greenhouse gases produced from burning fossil fuels. A host of other gases and particulate matter we put in the atmosphere degrade our air quality, too. A good example is the methane released from the thawing of the permafrost in the Arctic and sub-Arctic that is throwing more gas onto the fire—atmospheric warming. According to earth.stanford.edu, "methane is more than 80 times more potent than carbon dioxide in terms of warming the climate system."[25]

Air pollution and global climate change pose the greatest environmental health risk factor, and they are the most migratory. Regardless of the policies a government puts in place limiting fossil-fuel burning and particulate-matter emissions, the movement of our air does not respect human-made territorial boundaries. Being downwind from a neighboring air polluter is a physical problem requiring diplomatic efforts and intergovernmental action.

Even indoor air quality has become a critical issue, given the disregard until only recently for the chemical processing that many interior building materials and furnishings have used. In short, for most people of the planet today, there is something in the air, and it isn't a shared feeling about something good about to happen. Humankind has produced massive amounts of airborne gases and particulate matter that threaten lives.

Water is life. That statement is more than a Dakota Access Pipeline direct action political slogan—it is an existential fact. Yet water, like the land and air, for far too many on the planet is taken for granted, especially when about one-fourth of the eight billion people on the planet have no safe drinking water at home. Many argue that water scarcity is just as ominous an environmental threat as GCC. Ominous or not, most people are simply not paying attention, and this inattentiveness is directly related to the environmental crises of the land, air, and water life on the planet today.

One grotesque example of modern humankind's bad behavior with respect to water can be found in the single largest dump site on the planet: the Great Pacific Garbage Patch (GPGP) or Pacific trash vortex. According to the nonprofit The Ocean Cleanup, this concentration of trash, largely plastics, is about twice the size of Texas and, based on sampling, contains 1.8 trillion pieces of plastic with an estimated weight of 80,000 metric tons or 176,369,810 pounds. We might be thankful for the converging North Pacific Ocean currents, for this naturally occurring vortex traps the trash in this concentrated floating small-continent-size area.[26] It gives scientists, engineers, and policy makers a manageable area on which to focus clean-up and prevention activities. The GPGP provides a dramatic symbol of what is wrong on our planet today—too much trash, especially plastic.

Lakes, rivers, and naturally occurring ponds, do not fare much better when it comes to pollution. Unfortunately, all this eventually makes its way into our water, primarily through seepage and runoff (although winds can carry these chemicals, too). According to a recent study conducted by scientists with Greenpeace International and the Institute for Agriculture and Trade Policy (GRAIN):

> By way of massive government programmes and subsidies, the green revolution varieties quickly replaced local varieties and generated a huge boom in the global use of chemical fertilisers. They also kicked in a vicious cycle, in which more and more chemical fertilisers had to be applied to sustain yields. Today, only around 20–30% of the synthetic N fertilisers applied to fields are converted to foods, with the rest running off into water bodies and entering the environment as pollution . . . and causing a global crisis of algae blooms and oceanic "dead zones."[27]

Water is life and Mother Earth provides all that we need: but the problem is the way many of our humankind are living today. Remember the elder's admonition (see pp. 49–50) to respect the natural LAW—land, air, and water. As he so succinctly pointed out, if we disrespect the land, air, and water, humankind and the balance of the life on this planet will suffer. In the worst-case scenario, if we are too disrespectful to the land, air, and water, we might even receive a death sentence. Some of our human-kind seem to be testing this natural LAW right now—how far can we go in the extractive relations that define our industrial and postindustrial economies? We are pushing the limits of population, misconsumption, global burning of fossil fuels, and a host of other interrelated problems.

My fear is that as many start to recognize the problems we face, they will continue trying what *they think they know* to solve these problems. As the saying goes, we insanely, or maybe more appropriately, we ignorantly keep trying the same thing repeatedly and yet expect a different result each time. Humankind cannot keep thinking and acting the same way. Exercises of Indigenuity are attempts to think and behave differently in the world in which we—that is, life: the natural systems that support humankind and the different-than-human persons constituting the eco-kinship communities in which we participate—live. As the land, air, and water crises indicate, pollution problems are, for the most part, all about us. Except for earthquakes and volcanoes, the environmental pollution problems we are experiencing are very much human produced—they are an anthropogenic problem.

One might think that was good news: we created the problems, so we can fix them. However, the very kind of thinking that created these problems is the source of the environmental problems we now face. In an Indigenous way of thinking, the problems we face are not human problems, like that of our bipedal upright awkwardness—something we humankind universally share. The very human problem and the solutions that I suggest we explore reside in human cultures. The Western tradition at its core, built largely on ancient Greek and Christian religious ideas, promotes a universalizing and anthropocentric kind of thinking. It leads those who identify with that tradition—and the later, very "modern" Enlightenment term, *civilization*—to think their culture is the culture of civilization and progress: two of the most anthropocentric ideas on the planet.

The historic linkage in the West of culture with civilization leads inevitably to a perceived tension between nature and culture. The nature vs. culture dichotomy may be the most invidious dualism present in Western thought. It makes no sense unless one believes that, to borrow Hobbes's words, human life in a state of nature would be "solitary, poor, nasty, brutish, and short." Of course, the legacy of this unrealistic hypothetical conjecture is that humankind must control nature and, as Freud quite consistently argued in *Civilization and Its Discontents*, control our own human nature.

Suffice it to say, culture vs. nature—or humankind vs. nature—is a huge topic and one worthy of a book unto itself; however, we can say here that a radical difference between Western worldviews and Indigenous worldviews is found in the Western preoccupation with understanding themselves as made in God's image, given dominion over the Earth. As Genesis 1:28 states, "Be fruitful and multiply and fill the earth and subdue it, and have dominion over the fish of the sea and over the birds of the heavens and over every living thing that moves on the earth."

Indigenous worldviews in the Americas largely lack any sense of humankind being in charge of life on Earth or being in any sense superior in their likeness to God when compared to "the fish of the sea and . . . the birds of the heavens and . . . every living thing that moves on the earth." Instead, Indigenous worldviews (and this is a generalization, not a universal claim) see themselves as one small part of creation and certainly not in charge, as Vine Deloria, Jr. argued in *God Is Red* fifty years ago,

> The relationships that serve to form the unity of nature are of vastly more importance to most tribal religions. The Indian is confronted with a bountiful earth in which all things and experiences have a role to play. The task of the tribal religion, if such a religion can be said to have a task, is to determine the proper relationship that the people of the tribe must have with other living things and to develop the self-discipline within the tribal community so that man acts harmoniously with other creatures. The world that he experiences is dominated by the

> presence of power, the manifestation of life ener-
> gies, the whole life-flow of a creation. Recognition
> that the human beings hold an important place in
> such a creation is tempered by the thought that
> they are dependent on everything in creation for
> their existence.[28]

Indigenous Peoples acknowledge we live in what John Mohawk called the "complex web of life," and what scientists call the biosphere.

So many persons go about their everyday lives so immersed—deeply situated—in the digital representations of the world we live in, they begin to mistake their flat-screen representations of the world for the world itself. Their confusing of what they see and hear in this secondary-source reality with the world beyond and external to their flat-screens and virtual reality headsets is a major problem in the age of the Anthropocene.

Yes, many humans have now changed the basic systems of the planet. As a result of these Earth-system changes, the biosphere—the thin layer of life covering the Earth—is undergoing dramatic change. But this is old news and only half the story, for while most of the public have a vague and sometimes false notion of what GCC is, few know little about the technosphere or give it much, if any, thought. This is a huge problem (more about this later). However, one obvious part of the technosphere people in the US know very well is our love of automobiles—something sold to us very effectively, although a cursory review of surveys and articles related to Millennial and Gen Z car buying suggests this, too, may be changing.

Indeed, one of the challenges we have today is rethinking our modes of transportation. We built our relatively new cities in the US (when compared to Europe) on the idea that every American would own an automobile. Consequently, planners designed cities, and developers built them, on the unquestionable premise that people would move about in automobiles. Of course, internal congestion problems gave rise to the need for freeways, trafficways, and more highways that circumvented sometimes bisected cities as expressways.

In most cases, federally mandated environmental impact statements are anthropocentric documents that value the land, air, water, and the flora and fauna of proposed building locations with a human-scale measuring instrument as opposed to an ecosystem health index. Conveniently and sadly, if such overall ecosystem impacts and perturbations are raised by those who value ecological life systems, the response is that the place to be disturbed has already been disturbed by previous destructive activities. Considering this situation, it is not surprising, but nevertheless disappointing, that Haskell Indian Nations University in Kansas, her students, and allied environmental networks find themselves in a struggle to protect the Wakarusa River ecosystem, including wetlands, from a proposed South Lawrence Trafficway expansion.

This is not surprising, and it is disappointing, but above that the struggle is a stand—an "embodies" affirmation—for something beyond an anthropocentric idea of "progress" and development—ideas, indeed, ideologies that have a long history of coming at the expense of Peoples and Places with distinct personalities expressed in communities—lifeways and ecosystems. A stand for a place, the Haskell Wetlands and the larger Wakarusa riparian ecosystem and the Peoples, human and different-than-human persons, that have intrinsic value—not value measured by modern humankind's penchant for comfort, convenience, and capital gains.

A Wetland's Healing and Restoration: An Exercise of Indigenuity

The natural LAW affirms the deep relationality of the land, air, water, and all the life these elements support. When examining and discussing any of these members of the ecosystems and biomes of our Mother Earth, it is impossible to separate any one from the others. However, I would place the now three-decades-long effort to preserve the Wakarusa wetlands—aka Haskell wetlands, Baker wetlands, and Baker-Haskell wetlands—by Haskell Indian Nations University as a clear example of water Indigenuity in the face of present-day political and economic adversity. In the late 1980s and early 1990s, the City of Lawrence and Douglas County began a discussion about building a road on the south side of the city of Lawrence, Kansas. The argument made, almost four decades ago, in favor of a bypass was that with projected growth in Lawrence and Douglas County there would be a need to create a highway route to improve the commuter and large-truck traffic flow on K-10 between Lawrence and the south side of the greater Kansas City area. A route that would not go through the south side of Lawrence was favored. Thus was born the controversy over the South Lawrence Trafficway (SLT) and the mobilization of a Haskell student-led organization called the Wetlands Preservation Organization (WPO).

Despite alternate routes that would be less destructive to the wetlands, the route ultimately put forward by Douglas County and the Kansas Department of Transportation was a Thirty-Second Street alignment, which avoided crossing Haskell's campus (as an earlier proposed Thirty-First Street alignment had done). After several court actions and additional studies, the controversy over the SLT ended-up before the Tenth Circuit Court of Appeals in Denver. In July 2012, The Tenth Circuit ruled against the efforts of Haskell students, the WPO, alumni, and a host of Tribal Nation allies to protect the wetlands. The court's decision affirmed that the process used to select the Thirty-Second Street trafficway alignment was fair and compliant with federal law and process. To this day, the ruling says more about the low bar for environmental justice in highway construction than it does about the merits of the wetland defenders' arguments against bisecting one of the most unique wetlands in northeastern Kansas.

Conventional wisdom would say that Haskell lost the battle to save the wetlands. I think otherwise. We did lose the battle to keep a major trafficway from going through the Wakarusa wetlands. However, circumstances presented Haskell faculty and students, and our save the wetlands allies, with a heightened sense of responsibility toward the tremendously disturbed remaining wetlands. In fact, many of our students and faculty now felt, more than ever, attention needed to be paid to healing the sacred wetlands that remained under Haskell's care. In fact, with the vacating of the Thirty-First Street trafficway alignment, the county decided to remove Thirty-First Street, which existed on an easement granted by the Department of Interior in the 1950s and return the soil to grade after the pavement was removed. The bruised and scarred land was returned to Haskell in 2012, and with this return Haskell's effort for a natural process restoration began.

For the past decade, Dr. Bridget Chapin, professor of biology, has directed Indigenous undergraduate students in research around a restoration of what is now known as the

Haskell Wetlands. Usually at least two to three undergraduate students work with Dr. Chapin every summer. Their work and the way they have framed their activities to restore and revitalize a very disturbed ecosystem embody an exercise of Indigenuity.

How so? Unlike many projects that use a civil engineering definition of "wetlands," Dr. Chapin and her students measure quantities of water to fauna in soil saturation, employing an ecological definition. Their work embodies Indigenuity in its largely hands-off approach to observing the wetlands, watching its capacity to heal and let the land, water, plants, and animals tell them what she needs. No bulldozers or heavy earth-moving equipment has been used; instead, the approach is to learn from a greatly disturbed ecosystem community. In short, their research has focused on putting our human selves in *right relations* and affirming the natural LAW: our necessary maintenance of respectful and responsible relation with the land, air, water, and the life around us.

Their research has involved field studies to establish baseline vegetation data and macroinvertebrate and vertebrate animal population data in the four major water basins within the Haskell wetlands, with a focus on the distribution patterns and composition of plant species found within the removed roadbed. In the process, they have acquired knowledge of invasive and native plant species in the Haskell Wetlands and learned techniques for conducting plant surveys and collecting soil samples—all work done under the supervision of Dr. Chapin and collaborators Debbie Baker, associate director of the Central Plains Center for Bioassessment, and Don Huggins, director of the center. Their goal is to establish a long-term monitoring system for the flora and fauna of the wetlands.

Recently, students and faculty have set up cameras to document the animals in the Haskell Wetlands, monitoring their use of the underpasses that could represent wildlife corridors through barriers in this bisected wetland landscape. They have found that we have a lot more relatives in the wetlands than many would think, and they need some accommodations from us to remain there. The struggle to stand up for our relatives never stops, because those wanting more roads for humans never stops. In a response for public input on a new proposal to expand the SLT to four lanes and create easier access to it on the west side of Lawrence, Haskell's faculty-led Interdisciplinary Team wrote,

> The barrier the SLT created to movement southward by people and animals has limited Haskell community access to the full wetlands area that ranges all the way to the Wakarusa river. Underpasses at the east and west ends of 31st street are inadequate for people and animal passage to the

rest of this important formerly accessible wetland basin. Accommodations for animal passage have not been adequately incorporated into the SLT design along the entire length of the highway—in particular along the Haskell wetlands and along the west leg, and have not been considered during the SEIS [Supplemental Environmental Impact Statement] process. Animal-car incidents are an important safety hazard, and recent research using camera traps by faculty and students have shown significant use of the western underpass by animals (at least nine mammal species), indicating more are needed. We request an incorporation of animal and people passage features/elements into any future construction and would like to see additions of animal passage elements such as underpasses to existing sections of the SLT.[29]

It has been nearly half a century (1977) since Onondaga Faith-Keeper Oren Lyons gave a speech at the United Nations' International Conference on Discrimination Against Indigenous Populations in the Americas in Geneva, Switzerland. He noted, "I do not see a delegation for the Four Footed. I see no seat for the Eagles. We forget and we consider ourselves superior. But we are after all a mere part of Creation. And we must consider understanding where we are. And we stand somewhere between the mountain and the Ant. Somewhere and only there as part and parcel of the Creation."[30] Humility is a part of Indigenuity, for there is so much we don't know and so much yet to know. The work of Haskell students Nizhoni Woodie, Tasha Chenot, Ian Gambill, Courtney King, Kathy Littlebull, Jamie Colvin, Victoria Secondine, Dorothea Summers, Jamie Stallings, Rebecca Villalobos, Garrett Williams, and Joseph Zupan, to name a few, along with Dr. Chapin, speaks to the intrinsic value of learning from our relatives. Not surprisingly, priorities change when one moves from the paradigm of resource management to a worldview that emphasizes being in *right relations* with our different-than-human relatives with whom we share the planet.

V.

A Poem for Emma Olivia

A new life—a gift,
A reminder to think beyond our petty selves—
A gift that helps us understand
> *the fragile side of Beauty gives us strength*
> *and holds us, as we cradle her.*

A Beauty that makes us leave off hate and fear—
> *distrust and anger.*
A gift encouraging, we "take care."
A nativity story miraculous in many ways.
A story among hundreds
> *happening every minute every day.*

A gift that if accepted will give one pause
> *to ask what we might do*
> *with others still unknown,*
To ensure the Beauty we behold
> *while in an infant's grasp,*
Will grow and grow encircling everything and all.

A new life affirming the ancient wisdom
             that above all else we must give.
For to live in Beauty requires strength—
             a soulful power—
That we forget and, worse yet, often forfeit.

And in so doing disrespect the Beauty we received,
             that is the strength to struggle,
             for nothing less than justice
For every newborn child.

A gift that summons the recollection
             of the fragile Beauty we once all were.
A new life—a gift.

—DRW, February 27, 2015

A Grand Transformation Needed to Address Climate Change[31]

As a Tsoyoha (Yuchi)—child of the sun—one who understands my Yuchi People's existence—our earthly conception—as resulting from one drop of blood that fell from the sun to the Earth, it seems fitting for the progeny of such an event to speak about "the grand transformation needed to address climate change" to scientists, technicians, educators, and policy makers who study and think about the Earth, the sun, the moon, and the hundreds of billions of galaxies around us. In Tsoyoha traditions, every day is a gift. Life is a gift. The "grand transformation" may require, above all else, embodied gratitude and love in the work we must do to stop the incredible destruction underway—a "recollection of the fragile Beauty we once all were."

What is here offered is extended with humility, for my remarks are little more than a reporting out of Indigenous wisdom and knowledge from Indigenous wisdom-keepers, knowledge-holders, and the Earth herself. There is nothing original in my thinking, although the way Indigenous wisdom is here expressed in the colonizer's language is, for better or worse, mine. Many of my human teachers hold no academic credentials (though a few do), but what they all share is knowledge and wisdom born of a People's experience and mindfulness of landscapes and seascapes they have called home for centuries and millennia.

My words come with a deep concern, the kind of feeling impossible to shake that pushes itself unexpectedly into one's thoughts even in moments of joy and love: a nagging feeling that humankind has waited too long to address GCC. That stated, let me be clear: the situation is not hopeless; we still have the ability to address this global crisis. Therefore, I am not so pessimistic as to be a fatalist, nor am I interested in writing pessimistically as an act of intellectual narcissism.

I learned with the title of my last book that sometimes even brief declarations require considerable contextualization to be understood. My book, *Red Alert! Saving the Planet with Indigenous Knowledge* sounds like an extremely hubris-ridden anthropocentric declaration. Consequently, some of the folks I most wanted to read my book, since it makes a non-anthropocentric argument for environmental sanity, would not know that from the title and might well have been put off by such a seemingly anthropocentric and hubris-laden declaration.

But as those who read my book know, Indigenous knowledge, as I use the term, is a knowledge *coproduced* by humans, the landscapes and seascapes where one resides, and the life found therein. Indigenous knowledge, as I have received and understand it, is decidedly non-anthropocentric and non-anthropogenic.

Be careful with the words you use. My book title was a result of the feeling I had when participating in Al Gore's 07.07.07 global Save Our Selves (SOS) event to bring much needed attention to global climate change. I participated in the event with Gore at the Smithsonian National Museum of the American Indian on July 7, 2007. As a Tsoyaha (Yuchi) person I kept thinking how "saving ourselves" sounded so selfish, when "ourselves" was widely understood as humankind—like,

"Hey, don't worry about anyone else, let's focus on saving our human selves." Quite apart from this idea sounding unconscionable from a moral standpoint, it seemed to perpetuate the idea that humankind alone can solve our problems, and therein was the most serious problem with the event's name. With few exceptions, the way scientists and many activists talked made it clear that it was up to us—humankind alone— to solve the problem of GCC.

An anthropocentric formulation like "save ourselves" runs contrary to many Indigenous traditions. Indigenous Peoples around the world understand that our best teachers are the stars, sun, land, air, water, and our different-than-human natural kin: the plants and animals, living in the landscapes and seascapes we call home. In short, within a Tsoyaha worldview and those of many Indigenous Peoples around the world, the problems of modernity are bound up in the false and miseducative idea that our superior human rationality and intelligence gives us the vantage point from which we can manage the world.

The failure to understand the moral sphere of our existence as inclusive of the so-called natural world is foreign to most Indigenous traditions. Our human tendency to look only to ourselves for solutions to the practical problems of existence on this planet has led to a lack of attentiveness and mindfulness to what the land, air, water, and life of this Earth can teach humankind. The everyday environment for many living in modern industrial and postindustrial societies is an anthropocentric and anthropogenic room-full-of-mirrors environment. It is very difficult to see, hear, and directly experience the parts of creation that did not come from our minds and hands in the modern world.

Because we live for the most part in RFM environments that are designed, built, and, far too often, about just us—humankind—we have modern social institutions and organizations that are, not surprisingly, built on the mistaken idea that justice is about just us—humankind. All that many of us see today are reflections of our human selves in the RFM environments we inhabit, and it is not too far-fetched to suggest we have produced an insulated or isolated ignorance of the world we did not create. Because of this *room-full-of-mirrors* effect and the insulated/isolated ignorance it produces, even those that study the world not of our making—the so-called natural world—often think of it as full of objects and/or resources, unable to recognize a world full of relatives and teachers in the ancient classrooms out-of-doors.

The fact that a significant number of you recognize this point is hopeful and constitutes the basis for serious consideration. The Indigenous knowledges—I will use the plural—for strictly speaking the knowledges we now need are those so-called downscaled local knowledges about what is happening in the landscapes and seascapes that Indigenous

People know intimately from experience. The Indigenous knowledges of the Anishinaabe people of the Great Lakes Region are different from the knowledge the Dine' and the Pueblos have of the Desert Southwest, and this Southwest knowledge differs from the knowledge held by Peoples of the Great Plains of North America. In short, Indigenous knowledge is the domain of particular Peoples in particular places on the planet and, most importantly, the product of their life understood as part of a symbiotic nature culture nexus.

An Indigenous perspective is here offered—not the Indigenous perspective—but an understanding that I shared in 2009 in *Red Alert. Red Alert* recommended changes in how modern humankind thinks about our situation if we are to successfully address the "red alert" our planet—this beautiful blue-green Mother Earth—has been issuing for some time now. It is worth stating explicitly what a good number of folks reading this understand. The real problem facing planet Earth today is the way a good number of humankind think about it and our human place here, which results in bad, that is destructive, behavior.

The knowledge problem we currently face is essentially epistemic: what we think we know and how we think we know it. We desperately need traditional ecological knowledges now for their deeply relational and situational character. Modern objectivistic physical scientists, until very recently, understood knowledge itself as almost exclusively about objects—the world of atoms, particles, elements, molecules, and cells waiting to be discovered through data collection, experiment, dissection, and rigorous analytic procedures. Although field scientists and researchers appreciated the value of knowledge outside the bounds of the controlled experiment, the funders of scientific research made clear their preference for the lab sciences—those conducted in controlled environments. This prejudice tells us much about the dominant modern Western tradition's penchant for control and the mistaken notion that control is a prerequisite for knowing.

Given the gravity of our current Earth situation—a Mother Earth health crisis—four Indigenously inspired actions bear consideration. Consider the following points as four suggestions for Mother Earth actions promoting systems of life enhancement that Indigenous Peoples have learned from a careful attentiveness to a world not full of resources but rather one inhabited by relatives—plants, animals, and the land, air, and water.

Do not mistake the following for hyperbole: first, all four recommendations are examples of Indigenous Realism and an invitation to listen to People who hold deep knowledges and now are often directly experiencing the destructive and disruptive effects of GCC; and second, start the engagement in a manner unprecedented in the practice of geophysical sciences.

This will be difficult work, for the history of science is deeply intertwined with colonial practices of the dispossession of homelands and the attempted erasure of tribal identities and Indigenous peoplehood. But the interrelationship of colonization and science that Indigenous scientists are problematizing today requires serious examination and is quite deserving of an entire conference. With all of this in mind, here are the suggestions, I would like to share today.

First, listen to Indigenous Peoples. To successfully address geophysical effects of climate change we must launch a systemic effort to create a cultural climate change. As the name of this age of Anthropocene denotes, the present physical GCC crisis is anthropogenic. And herein lies our present predicament: the best physical science may go a long way toward helping us understand the physical changes we are observing and might expect to see in the future, but addressing this physical climate change problem at its source will require a cultural climate change—a paradigm shift. In short, the GCC crisis now facing us is at its root a worldview problem when examined through an Indigenous lens.

If it is true that "one cannot fix or solve problems with the same kind of thinking that created them," then we should all be thankful that Indigenous Peoples, despite the depredations of modernity and civilization, still hold a tremendous amount of embodied knowledge in their lifeways. And this knowledge represents very different ways of thinking than those that produced the threatening global climate change we're now experiencing. Suffice it to say that traditional Indigenous knowledge systems are especially useful now because they constitute knowledges held by Peoples who never thought in boxes nor did their life's work in silos.

It is time to listen to Indigenous voices because we need a cultural climate change.

Second, the cultural climate change we need entails losing the largely anthropocentric modern worldview substituting instead an Indigenous Peoples–informed geo-eco-cultural, or Gaia-cultural, worldview where our cultures are once again framed and understood as inextricably linked to a nature culture nexus. The miseducative decoupling of nature and culture has played a major role in creating the crisis we now face. Tribal Indigenous cultures embody this NCN. Modern humankind has much to learn from the examination of the NCN of our human existence.

In place of an essentially modern anthropocentric worldview, we now must foster something widely found in Indigenous tribal Peoples' worldviews: a non-anthropocentric worldview that situates our human place in the world as but one small, albeit powerful, part of larger geo-eco-cultural landscapes and seascapes. This dethroning of our human selves, walking away from measurements of progress that are entirely anthropocentric, will be critical to successfully address GCC. Humans are hardly the measure of all things, and behaving as if we are has brought us, thus far, to the life-threatening age of the Anthropocene.

For Indigenous tribal thinkers, the landscapes, seascapes, and cultural features of our worldviews—that is, the material, organizational, behavioral, symbolic, and linguistic features— were tacitly understood as repositories of pluridimensional relationships that embodied knowledge and pluripotency with respect to knowledges as relationships changed. In this sense the "things" old-fashioned scientists once observed, collected, and studied were never observed and understood by Indigenous knowledge-holders in that discrete, objective manner. Rather, Indigenous knowledges were and remain, above all else, relational in character.

Third, because there are Indigenous Peoples on this beautiful blue-green planet who can offer some useful insight into what some features of a cultural climate change could be, we must build respectful and responsible collaborations. The bad news is our numbers are small and sadly declining in many places on the planet due to the dominant modern worldview that created the climate crisis. Also, remember that Indigenous People who hold these knowledges do so as lifeways, so much of what you expect of a good partnership will require a tremendous change—indeed accommodation—on the part of scientists used to collecting knowledge. Be prepared to spend your time on their lands building relationships and trust to demonstrate a nonextractive respect of the knowledges shared.

But there is the good news, too: a significant number of scientists are now doing their work using theories, models, and research methods that recognize understanding GCC will require a fundamentally complex relational understanding of its geophysical processes, including human behavior and lifeways. It is the deeply relational and process-oriented character of GCC research that makes respectful engagement with Indigenous Peoples particularly opportune. Both the 2006 formation of the tribal college and university–centered American Indian and Alaska Native Climate Change Working Group, now known as the Indigenous Peoples Climate Change Working Group, and a 2012 convening of the University Center for Atmospheric Research that supported Rising Voices activities and now the Rising Voices Center, embody the value of bringing TEKs and their Indigenous knowledge-holders and communities together with leading scientific organizations and climate scientists. Engagement is the work that must now be undertaken. It is hard work. Too few physical scientists get paid to build relationships with Places and Peoples, and this must change.

Fourth, as a part of this necessary cultural climate change, it is time for humankind to consider moving from a worldview dominated by thinking about how we might better use "our" resources. We need to take a much more Indigenous and honestly scientific view of the land, air, water, and life all three support by viewing our challenge as learning to live well among relatives, not resources.

Indigenous knowledges are the antidote to the destructive age of the Anthropocene we are living in. Indigenous knowledges result from a coproduction of knowledge that understands the world's plants, animals, and geophysical features as our teachers in "classrooms" out-of-doors. The earth's geophysical and ecological systems can teach us about how we, humankind, might live more respectfully and responsibly in the landscapes and seascapes that all of humankind needs to understand as our homelands. It is time—right now—to promote system-of-life enhancement on this beautiful Mother Earth.

Maybe we have time to back off the largely anthropocentric notion of progress, which measures everything in terms of our human comfort, convenience, and capital gains, to a more kin-centric view of life on this planet and think about improvement as promoting systems of life enhancement. If we do, we might move away from destructive relations and fear that create the need for building activities around food, water, and housing security and ultimately a Department of Homeland security. When I think about our children and grandchildren as many Indigenous Peoples do, seven generations into the future, I want instead to foster a culture of *Homeland Maturity* for humankind and our different-than-human natural relatives.

In short, it is now time to consider the usefulness of a systemic paradigm shift that emphasizes at once a more integrated, interrelated, and complex system of Earth and space science that allows for the production of knowledge in places where we cannot employ the classic scientific method of the controlled experiment. We must encourage approaches that include Indigenous knowledges emergent from the symbiotic relationship of Peoples and Places. Let's become good relatives to the life we share with our many relatives on this planet and act in such a way that we will be remembered as good ancestors for future generations.

Science is a multifaceted process bringing to bear different kinds of observations, histories, and technologies to the understanding of natural phenomena. Diversifying ways of knowing serves to strengthen that understanding. Bringing together governmental policy with academic and tribal perspectives, such as combining remote sensing data with in-situ, on-the-ground knowledges held by Indigenous Peoples, is critical. When science ignores Indigenous perspectives, scientific understanding and outcomes are compromised through loss of designs and solutions never considered. Building collaborations with sovereign Tribal Nations, Tribal colleges and universities, and communities requires an emphasis on respectful and responsible *right relations* as well as Indigenous historical and cultural practices. In conclusion, in the context of our current global climate crisis it is time for humankind to get *this* right. We, humans, cannot afford to get this wrong.

VI.

Out of Doors

My living room is out of doors.
Inside walls it's hard to breath.
Inside doors it's hard to live.

Doors and walls serve some good
Their utility is understood.
Our fragile species often need reprieve
From hot and cold—from wind and wet—
But seldom from the wild.
For on the whole, when all is said
The wild brings life from what is dead.

My living room is out of doors.
A new carpet of decaying leaves is laid.
No walls needed. No walls to paint.

For everywhere I look new scenes appear
No need for hanging pictures here
For the painter's canvas is everywhere

I have both heat and cold—
No utility bills to pay.
No thermostat to set—
No dimming switch for light control
Daily I have light and dark—year-round.

My living room is out of doors.
Oh the decorator can be testy and temperamental at times.
She has designs at many levels of all kinds.

Her aesthetic is full of rhythms expressed in colors
that often rhyme.
She is time—for those in need of order.
She is space—for those who dream.
She offers places so we can have homes.

My living room is out of doors.
And so I ask where is yours?
Interiors and exteriors—I have high regard.
But when artificial spaces oppress,
I suggest, step inside my living room out of doors
The beauty is . . . it is yours.

—DRW, October 10, 2013–November 12, 2016

Finding Our Home with
Mother Earth

Yes, it is hard to state where *we* stand right now. *We*, to be precise, those of us inhabiting industrial and post-industrial societies, are constantly on the move. Even during the Covid-19 pandemic when we were advised to stay home and stay safe, our bodies may have been stationary, but our attention was elsewhere: many were occupied by virtual spaces neither here nor there, but everywhere and nowhere.

When sheltering in place during a global pandemic, too few of us developed a deeper appreciation or mindfulness to/ of the place where we sheltered. More likely we easily got lured into an internet outer pace, "where" sadly, with consequences yet unknown, even daydreaming has been replaced by live streaming.

It is difficult to make a stand, to take a "grounded" posi-tion if one is constantly moving, or, worse yet, if due to the media saturation many face today, *we are not really there when we are anywhere*—even our residential addresses.

The environments we inhabit in industrial and postindus-trial societies produce an effect equivalent to living in a room full of mirrors—the RFM effect, where all we experience is reflec-tions of ourselves. In the first instance, ourselves embodied and projected in our human creations. At a second, deeper level, given the commercial-commodity culture we find ourselves immersed within, we mistakenly grant a power independent of our human selves to these commodity creations. However, our RFM is not only filled with ordinary mirrors but also mirrors in which our images are distorted: one moment exaggerated and the next drastically diminished as in a carnival fun house or house of horror.

Despite its duly attested comfort and convenience, dwelling in the US room full of mirrors, comes at a high price—literally and figuratively. Humankind *experiences* a sort of *mis-orientation*—not merely a false consciousness—that manifests itself in all kinds of social and psychological pathologies amidst this culture of technological narcissism. Being "normal" in this room full of mirrors results in the development of an adaptive mis-orientation—mis-orientation in the sense that our attention is completely drawn away from the biosphere in which our rooms are situated. Instead, our attention is directed toward our own inventions. Immersed in modern or postmodern societies, all most of us see is ourselves in the innovations and technologies that create the places and the virtual information technology (IT) spaces where we increasingly spend our waking hours. I leave it to the postmodernists to tell me if they hear echoes of Baudrillard in this experiential assessment. I am working with primary sources—my own sense experiences, and that is what matters.

Indeed, as advertisers have clearly discovered, even our self-worth is today valued in terms of the technological innovations we own and deploy. Our attention is taken from the physical place and space where one is geospatially located to a cyberspace "place." What this means in terms of human experience can hardly be fathomed. Our sense experience is channeled and dislocated from that "present" place and space where we are physically and spiritually grounded, and where our species has evolved and resided for at least five million years, to a cyberspace where our attention is directed and our experience is truncated and flattened into the screens through which many on the planet now see—experience?—the world.

Unlike the printed word that allows us to be transported to somewhere or someplace in our imagination, the HD images we perceive in the IT, "www.world," where many minds are "presently" occupied, are the creation of someone else's design work and imagination. This explains why the HD and/or 3D movie is never as good as the book, where characters are cast and the narrative and scenes are staged in our mind—our imagination. Consequently, the movie is seldom as we thought it would be. How could it be? It is necessary to consider this Oz-like view of experience—pay no attention to the man behind the curtain—as the IT–social media reality increasingly constituting the bulk of young people's experience in modern societies.

What happens when one calls on a person's experience to inform their understanding of the world only to find out most of their experience is quite literally blogs, web pages, YouTube, Facebook, Tinder, Twitter, streaming media, and so on. They are indeed paying attention, but to what and where? And how does one do ground-truthing work in such an environment? What happens when we call on a person's environmental awareness, and their environment is overwhelming populated with flat-screen cyberspace experience? Again, I will plead ignorance to what cultural geographers, historians, and scientists are doing with all this, but the mapping of this IT landscape feature of the technosphere is well underway, I am sure. The challenge is thinking about how we might understand the cyberspace landscape without treating it as the "other" landscape—is that even possible? Does it make *sense*?

In the IT realm of the technosphere, experiential learning means something totally different today—what we experience now seems projected from secondary sources. Do life lessons—those insights we gain through experience—really mean the same thing they once did when we no longer rely on our own primary sources, on our direct, nontechnology-mediated experience, for the majority of our life experience?

With respect to the exponential growth of the internet and "www-driven" IT and social-media spaces where an increasing amount of time is spent, the really radical—indeed revolutionary—feature of this technology is that there is no there . . . there—in any kind of physical, geographical sense. What we now have are www.addresses that take us to media spaces where our mind and body are stimulated by "who knows who?" at "who knows where?" And we call this being connected. Experience in this flat-screen reality is now here, there, everywhere, and nowhere.

This adaptive mis-orientation operates at four levels. Most fundamentally it leads to the mistaken idea that human cultures can operate relatively autonomously from landscapes and seascapes: an idea that has worked short-term, but now seems highly problematic when one factors in the issue of sustainability.

Second, and precisely because of the modern infatuation with scientific and technical interventions in natural phenomena, humankind seems to increasingly see the balance of nature beyond us, so wanting and in need of improvement that a sort of technological manifest destiny compels us to seek technological modification and control of nature.

Third, because our urban and suburban landscapes are so heavily marked by the human hand, it creates a mistaken view that real nature exists only in national parks and wilderness areas. Our human-made environment is so dominating in the modern-industrial (MI) and postindustrial (PI) societies that, even when people step outside interior spaces, it is difficult to perceive the other-than-human features of the Earth enveloping them. It is mistaken to think that nature is nonexistent inside the walls of our schools, offices, and homes. It is doubly problematic to forget that life pulses in the environment right outside our interior spaces. Even sitting on the seventh floor of a hotel one block off the so-called Magnificent Mile in downtown Chicago, the natural world—the land, air, and water—surrounds us, although it is heavily camouflaged and shaped by humans.

Fourth, and possibly most dangerously, the RFM society we inhabit leads individuals in MI-societies and PI-societies to see their own selves as essentially a physical apparatus that can be improved through all manner of technologies and design procedures. In our anthropocentric self-consciousness we anoint ourselves as the creator and the prime mover of creation and in startling, contradictory fashion submit our lives to the technological enslavement of human-produced machines. Intoxicated with our accomplishments and mis-oriented in our focus, the most technologically advanced of our species constantly mis-identifies the central features of the challenges facing the planet at the beginning of the twenty-first century. Our humanity is defined by and understood as technology/machine. Yet we are so much more than the machines we make and employ.

Evidence of our failure to see our human cultures as both the source and solution for the many life-threatening events is everywhere. Nowhere can this be seen more clearly than in the commercial media, which, in a sense, constitutes the newest and ultimate human-made IT space many humans—especially young people—now inhabit.

Two examples of the way in which many in modern societies are *occupied* by technology stand out. First are the popular, award-winning advertisements by IBM and Dow Chemical. Both illustrate our current human mis-orientation toward problems now facing the planet. The IBM commercial goes like this: "Help us build a smarter planet." Did I miss something? When did the planet get dumb? Help "us"—who? IBM? They want you and me to be IBMers and help them build a smarter planet? I ask myself again—the planet is not smart enough?

The problem is not the planet. I would settle for improving the general level of intelligence of the species that would issue such a hubris-ridden call to action. The major problem the planet is facing is not the ignorance or stupidity of the planet; rather, it is those who see the problem as one to be fixed by technology. The largest problems facing the planet today are directly linked to earlier applications of technologies we employed to make the planet a better place for us—humankind.

Dow Chemical's "human element" commercials are a good example of how beautiful photography (especially the images of Indigenous Peoples), a sanguine voice, and a good storyline can sell us a fable, a fiction, as "truth." Dow's commercials tell us that this beautiful world we inhabit is made up of chemicals—which is true—but it implies that this beautiful world has only been threatened because the periodic table is missing one key element: the "human element." Unfortunately, Dow chemical's history with respect to pollution and death suggests otherwise. Dow's record with respect to napalm, dioxin, and Agent Orange alone suggests that a very modern, rational, resource-oriented view of life on the planet has guided their work.

In short, when humans using Dow chemicals come to the forest, the rivers, and grasslands, much of the different-than-human natural life, if they could speak our human languages, might reasonably shout, "Go away, please go away!" The modern rational human element has hardly been missing. As for compassion and concern just for humans, even that seems to be mitigated by a concern for profits and winning wars, even if winning means ecological devastation.

Let's be clear, humankind per se is not the problem, nor is technology, nor is the planet. The problem is humans employing technologies with little regard to how their use will impact the diverse environments and ecosystems that constitute that thin layer of life we, humankind, inhabit: our Mother Earth's biosphere. Clare Miflin, an architect and certified biomimicry professional, eloquently summed up an ancient piece of Indigenous wisdom. She wrote, "But waste is not present in nature; it is a human design flaw. Waste is the product of a linear system: Materials are extracted from the earth, processed and used, often very briefly, before being thrown out. Ecosystems, though, have circular systems: Materials are used and recycled in constant loops."[32]

We suffer today primarily from what I previously called an *insulated ignorance*. Many of us in the US spend our time inside insulated homes, and most spend more time in these kinds of human-engineered and -designed environments than out-of-doors. The result of life in these room-full-of-mirrors environments is insulated ignorance.

The first challenge educators today must address is how to rethink education—how we can do education out-of-doors? We must start paying attention to the world around us. We have indeed inculcated a sort of *insulated ignorance* with the way we live today. I mean this in a fundamentally experiential sense.

Take Education Out-of-Doors

The best way to overcome the negative features of this age of the Anthropocene, this human-centered age of Earth history, is to reengage with the life systems that we are fundamentally changing with little regard for the larger Earth-system consequences. This reengagement is something that every educator can and must do. If we get students out-of-doors, questions will emerge about the land, air, and water: Why do we have certain areas in cities that flood, and what is the cause? Where does our drinking water come from? Where does our wastewater end up? How do we or should we even capture rainwater? What do we do in terms of improving our ability to responsibly use water? This last question is a fundamental one. We could ask similar questions about land use.

Again, these questions are all related, and this is the ultimate point: when we get outside of our educational institutions, we walk outside the silos of knowledge in the academy and start tackling practical everyday problems. We seldom ask what "disciplines" we are going to seek to help us solve these everyday problems. For example, there are practical problems of transportation, how we are going to feed ourselves, where we are going to live, and what consumer choices we are going to make. These are all interrelated, but somehow, we forget this interrelatedness once we move into institutions of higher education.

The existential threat of the GCC is the result of a natural *experiential deficit crisis* some humans have produced. We spend so much time inside human-designed RFM environments that we have literally insulated ourselves into ignorance. To create the cultural climate change we need, we must address the *insulated ignorance* that the RFM produces. We must dramatically rethink education.

If we are going to teach about the land, air, water, and life systems we are a part of, the best place to do it is to step right outside our human-made environments and start asking questions about how we could live better here—in the land-scape and natural environment where we find ourselves daily. There is nothing romantic about this activity. As I noted earlier, it is, in fact, Indigenous Realism. The practical effi-cacy of the knowledge and wisdom that Indigenous People have is the result of living in places over long periods of time where knowledge about those places was intergenerationally handed down—and much of this knowledge is empirical and experiential. The First Peoples of this land had a very deep spatial experiential knowledge of what worked well in their homelands and what did not. My suggestion is that if we take education out-of-doors and see what the planet herself can teach us, we just might learn something about what it means to become more competent and mature human beings.

In our teaching we must be careful not to induce or exacerbate climate anxiety—a real condition in which many people become anxious and fearful about the future given what they hear it might look like in the face of climate change. It is extremely important that we be sensitive to this situation and about how we teach children and young folks about climate change. We must be mindful of this situation, be honest about the condition we are creating; yet we must provide some advice for practical activities that can help us make the future less menacing than if we simply succumb to fear and hopelessness.

When we step outside our human-built environment, and are outside long enough, we get the secondary benefit of recognizing how small we are in this great cosmos in which we participate. It gives us the opportunity to be in *right relationship* with the balance of creation. As I've noted, by right relation or relationship, I mean assuming a position of humility about power and knowing that results in mindfulness regarding our activities and behavior: humility expressed in having a worldview that is decidedly non-anthropocentric. The world does not, in fact, revolve around us. Inculcating humility is critical if we are to let Mother Earth teach us, and easy to come by if we ponder the expansive character of the cosmos.

I like Paolo Freire's Introduction in his follow-up book to *The Pedagogy of the Oppressed*, *The Pedagogy of Hope*, where he talks about hope as being an ontological (a real) condition.[33] Freire addresses how we must have hope when we are facing very real problems. We are not going to underestimate and sugarcoat the threat of GCC, but we must use this opportunity to talk about solutions—actions and activities students can do. Minus that work, students will likely be left with a sense of hopelessness.

So, how do we talk about hope? How do we talk about giving students hope in a world where their and our own bandwidth might be consumed with any number of crises—an economic crisis, a pandemic crisis, a governmental crisis, an education crisis, or a justice crisis? How do we ask people to think about a climate crisis, too? It is so easy to overwhelm ourselves and certainly students with these multiple levels of crises. After all, we have only so much mental capacity available to deal with these things. So, let's be mindful of our bandwidth issues in whatever we do.

As I've noted, we must consider a fundamental reframing, a paradigm shift—a cultural climate change—of how we will discuss the issue of GCC. This paradigm shift will allow us to tie all these different threads together. The first thread is disabusing ourselves of an anthropocentric worldview: the idea that "it is all about us." The second is the recognition that the balance of creation, the parts of the physical world that we had no hand in shaping are not resources but instead are relatives, as many Indigenous Peoples understand the plants, animals, land, air, and water to be.

Think of how shifting away from thinking that we live in a world full of resources to one where we live in a world full of relatives would fundamentally change attitudes and actions with respect to the natural world. This relational, or relationship-driven, view is much more consistent with the modern ideas of evolution, ecology, convergence science, and the way many of us talk about transdisciplinary science. To understand the wicked-complex problems we face, we must understand relations and relationships. Climate change is a good example here because of the complexity of this global phenomenon. Climate change requires a paradigm that understands relationships and processes and sees that understanding as a strength.

This relationship-defined worldview explains why in many tribal traditions of governance, rights are understood as hollow unless coupled with unalienable responsibilities. When we live among resources, all we do is argue about whose right it is to use them. When we live among relatives, we must ask ourselves: what is our responsibility to those different-than-human relatives?

If we make this paradigm shift, we can then shift the current discussion about sustainability, which unfortunately gets overburdened addressing the greenwashing of corporate sustainability agendas, to a discussion about ecological life-system resilience. Almost every corporation on the planet now has a sustainability platform, including some of the most damaging industries to the Earth. The question is, what are they trying to sustain?

Instead, we should talk about resilience, but resilience as more than being able to adapt, respond, and bounce back. We must think about a kind of *resilience plus*. With all the difficulties facing us, we do not want to just go back to where we were. We must create something more enriching to life on the planet. Our work is to start building examples of what systems of life enhancement, or *resilience plus*, look like.

Given its deep historical "positive" connotations, few folks in modern society want to be against progress. Nevertheless, "progress" as it has been defined is a very anthropocentric term, and I am not sure it can be redefined minus its deep anthropocentric baggage. Regardless, we must begin clearly articulating and creating systems of life enhancement—not just for our human selves, but for all life, all the relatives with whom we share this Mother Earth. This is Indigenous Realism.

Upper-administration support to provide incentives to design the curricula and courses students need within our institutions of education is critical. Such support is necessary, both for teachers in K–12 education and faculty in post-secondary institutions, to be able to work across disciplines in an interdisciplinary fashion. Faculty, too, must be the leaders in this institutional change.

In an era of limited budgets, we provide very little incentive for people to cross disciplinary boundaries in their teaching. We need a major push to get our colleges and universities to "walk the talk" about interdisciplinary teaching and research. Those in public higher education must work within legislatures, faculty senates, and boards of regents to get administrators to commit to, if not adding to their budget, dollars to support interdisciplinary teaching. Minus this institutional commitment it is difficult to get this work done.

We must close the gap between real-world problems and our siloed disciplinary institutions. Suppose we designed a course about climate change, we would at minimum want someone from social sciences, the school of business/management, environmental science, and earth sciences. The wicked part of climate change is that all these departments and disciplines are entangled in such a manner that it takes discussion between and across areas to solve this problem. All these phenomena are interrelated, and giving experts the opportunity to explore the nature of these relationships and involve students is crucial to changing the way we think about many problems today.

It is imperative that the teaching and research include tribal and community knowledge-holders, ultimately recognizing that we still have so much to learn from them. This is a good way to do the ground-truthing of problems and solutions. Minus these on-the-ground experts, we often present the problems we want to address as generic abstractions, frequently making our proposed solutions unworkable. If we can demonstrate to students that climate change is not an abstraction but instead is directly related to where they live and go to school, and most importantly, how they live, we can plant the seeds for real change. We must seize the opportunity of preparing students to get on the ground in communities to address the practical climate change problems facing them.

While we need big-picture climate modelers, there is a lot that can be done on the ground at the community level. Again, we must get students out-of-doors. We should promote project-based and hands-on learning that identify those real challenges our communities face, and then work with students to start figuring out how to understand these problems. We must teach students how to work in teams, analyze problems, model solutions, and make changes to existing systems. And here is the good news, if we can accomplish this work, we will not have to live in a world full of fear anymore.

The horror of 9/11 resulted in the creation of a whole new government agency: the Department of Homeland Security. Post 9/11, a very real challenge is to not let fear dominate our lives. People talk about food security, housing security, economic security, and so forth. In our resource-filled world, we are constantly afraid of losing or having a lack of resources. But what or whom are we afraid of? I suggest that by moving from a worldview where the world is understood as full of resources to one where the world is full of relatives, from a preoccupation with rights to a counterbalancing respect for responsibilities, we can move away from questions of mere sustainability to *resilience plus*.

With respect to incorporating Indigenous research methods in this work, the most important research skills reside in communication—simply talking and listening to others.

And of the two skills, active listening is far and away the most important. Both are a subset of the attitude of attentiveness or mindfulness about our situation—our place in this world. In my book with Vine Deloria, Jr., *Power and Place: Indian Education in America*, I referred to this as *synthetic attentiveness*—the ability to be aware without consciously thinking about needing to be aware of ourselves in relationship to others and the world around us.[34] This characteristic of human maturity may be what is most threatened in the algorithm-driven, smart-phone reality that grabs our attention. It also helps us understand why education, now more than ever, requires a reengagement with the out-of-doors and the world beyond the flat screens of our technological devices. This shift to an ability to be mindful, fully aware, and sensitive to the world in which we live is the key to true resilience—*resilience plus*.

As I noted earlier, *resilience plus* thinking and activity suggests we can co-create systems of life enhancement by partnering with the natural world as opposed to working "on" or "with" nature. By exercising ancient tribal wisdom and knowledge to solve contemporary problems—Indigenuity— my hope is that our children and grandchildren will not live in a fear-driven world but rather one that fosters a sense of *Homeland Maturity*. Ultimately, *Homeland Maturity* is what the planet needs right now: human beings who are thinking about something other than themselves, and human beings who are going to let our mother, the Earth, teach us how to be more competent, mature humans.

It is time to listen to Indigenous Peoples on the planet and hope that exercises of Indigenuity might help us make life with our Mother Earth better. As the wise elder reminded those of us present three decades at an intertribal GIS meeting, if we disrespect the land, air, and water, the consequences may be fatal for ourselves and many of our different-than-human relatives. It is time to learn the lessons of our mother to address problems that cannot be solved with the same kind of thinking that created them. It is time to exercise some long overdue ***Indigenuity***.

Notes

1. World Wildlife Fund, "10 Myths About Climate Change," https://www.wwf.org.uk/updates/here-are-10-myths-about-climate-change.

2. Shannon Hall, "Exxon Knew About Climate Change Almost 40 Years Ago," *Scientific American*, October 26, 2015, https://www.scientificamerican.com/article/exxon-knew-about-climate-change-almost-40-years-ago/.

3. Rick Potts, "Living in the Anthropocene: Being Human in the Age of Humans," *National Museum of the American Indian Magazine*14, no. 4 (2013): 27–31.

4. "Calculating Migration Expectancy Using ACS Data," December 23, 2021, https://www.census.gov/topics/population/migration/guidance/calculating-migration-expectancy.html.

5. Neil E. Klepeis et al. "The National Human Activity Pattern Survey (NHAPS): A Resource for Assessing Exposure to Environmental Pollutants," https://eta-publications.lbl.gov/sites/default/files/lbnl-47713.pdf.

6. Daniel R. Wildcat, *Red Alert! Saving the Planet with Indigenous Knowledge* (Golden, CO: Fulcrum Publishing, 2009).

7. See Brian Swann's Introduction to the book of that title (*Smoothing the Ground: Essays on Native American Oral Literature*, University of California Press, 1983). My thought is of "smoothing the ground" as akin to cleaning or preparing the ground for ceremony or a sacred act.

8. For the United Nations Declaration on the Rights of Indigenous Peoples, see UNDRIP_E_web.pdf.

9. G. Albrecht, G. M. Sartore, L. Connor, N. Higginbotham, S. Freeman, B. Kelly, H. Stain, A. Tonna, and G. Pollard, "Solastalgia: The Distress Caused by Environmental Change," *Australasian Psychiatry* (2007):15 Suppl 1:S95-8. doi: 10.1080/10398560701701288. PMID: 18027145.

10. For a deeper discussion of Bob Thomas and Peoplehood, see Tom Holm, J. Diane Pearson, and Ben Chavis. "Peoplehood: A Model for the Extension of Sovereignty in American Indian Studies." *Wicazo Sa Review* 18, no. 1 (Spring 2003): 7–24, or https://www.jstor.org/

stable/1409431. For more on how power and place equal personality, see Vine Deloria, Jr. and Daniel R. Wildcat, *Power and Place: Indian Education in America* (Golden, CO: Fulcrum Publishing, 2001).

11. For John Mohawk, "How the Conquest of Indigenous Peoples Parallels the Conquest of Nature," see the Schumacher Center for a New Economics (centerforneweconomics.org).

12. Robin Wall Kimmerer, *Braiding Sweetgrass: Indigenous Wisdom, Scientific Knowledge, and the Teachings of Plants* (Minneapolis: Milkweed Editions, 2015).

13. Vine Deloria, Jr., *God Is Red: A Native View of Religion* (Wheat Ridge, CO: Fulcrum Publishing, 2023).

14. N. Scott Momaday, *The Way to Rainy Mountain* (Albuquerque: University of New Mexico Press, 1976).

15. Keith H. Basso, *Wisdom Sits in Places: Landscape and Language Among the Western Apache* (Albuquerque: University of New Mexico Press, 1996).

16. Alan Watts, *Nature, Man and Woman* (New York: Random House, 1988).

17. Kimmerer, *Braiding Sweetgrass*, 9.

18. Frank J. Popper and Deborah E. Popper, 1994. "Great Plains: Checkered Past, Hopeful Future," *Forum for Applied Research and Public Policy* 9, no. 4 (1994): 89–100, Tennessee Valley Authority.

19. R. E. A. Almond, M. Grooten, D. Juffe Bignoli, and T. Petersen, eds., *Living Planet 2022—Building a Naturepositive Society* (Gland, Switzerland: World Wildlife Fund, 2022).

20. Vine Deloria, Jr., *The World We Used to Live In: Remembering the Powers of the Medicine Men* (Golden, CO: Fulcrum Publishing, 2009).

21. National Park Service, "Effigy Mounds National Monument Becomes a Tribal Sister Park to Ioway Tribal National Park," November 24, 2022, https://www.nationalparkstraveler.org/2022/11/effigy-mounds-national-monument-becomes-tribal-sister-park-io-way-tribal-national-park.

22. Lance Foster, *The National Parks Traveler* podcast, 2021, https://www.nationalparkstraveler.org/podcast/2021-01-31-national-parks-traveler-episode-103-ioway-tribal-national-park.

23. Kirkpatrick Sale, *The Conquest of Paradise: Christopher Columbus and the Columbian Legacy* (New York: Knopf Publishing Group, 1990).

24. Deloria, Jr., *God Is Red*, 274.

25. Josie Garthwaite, "Methane and Climate Change," November 2, 2021, https://earth.stanford.edu/news/methane-and-climate-change.

26. The Ocean Cleanup, "The Great Pacific Garbage Patch," https://theoceancleanup.com/great-pacific-garbage-patch/.

27. GRAIN, "New Research Shows 50 Year Binge on Chemical Fertilisers Must End to Address Climate Crisis," November 1, 2021, https://grain.org/en/article/6761-new-research-shows-50-year-binge-on-chemical-fertilisers-must-end-to-address-the-climate-crisis#:~:text=Blog-,New%20research%20shows%2050%20year%20binge%20on%20chemical%20fertilisers,to%20address%20the%20climate%20crisis&text=The%20rising%20costs%20of%20synthetic,a%20catastrophic%20global%20ood%20crisis.

28. Deloria, Jr., *God Is Red*.

29. From a letter authored by the Haskell Indian Nations Interdisciplinary Team, September 30, 2021. Kansas Department of Transportation c/o Kris Norton, PE Division of Program and Project Management Bioscience and Technology Business Center, 2029 Becker Drive, Suite 236, Lawrence, KS 66047.

30. See Elisabeth Oseanita Pukan, "Haudenosaunee Indigenous Knowledge as Reflected in Oren Lyons' 'Where Is the Eagle Seat?' An Oration to the United Nations," https://e-journal.usd.ac.id/index.php/JOLL/article/viewFile/359/306.

31. This section is based on my presentation, "The Grand Transformation Needed to Address Climate Change," at the annual American Geophysical Union Fall Meeting in New Orleans, Louisiana, on December 14, 2021.

32. Clare Miflin, "If Nature Doesn't Need Trash, Neither Do We," Grist, October 24, 2018, https://grist.org/article/if-nature-doesnt-need-trash-neither-do-we/.

33. Paulo Freire and Ana Maria Ara, *Pedagogy of Hope: Reliving Pedagogy of the Oppressed* (London: Continuum International Publishing Group, 1997).

34. Deloria, Jr. and Wildcat, *Power and Place*.

Further Reading

Capra, F. *The Web of Life: A New Scientific Understanding of Living Systems*. New York: Anchor Books, 1996.

Deloria, V. *God Is Red: A Native View of Religion*. Wheat Ridge, CO: Fulcrum Publishing, 2023.

Deloria, V. *The Metaphysics of Modern Existence*. Golden, CO: Fulcrum Publishing, 2012.

Deloria, V., and J. Treat. *For This Land: Writings on Religion in America*. London: Routledge, 1999.

Deloria, V., and D. Wildcat. *Power and Place: Indian Education in America*. Golden, CO: Fulcrum Publishing, 2001.

Kimmerer, R. W. *Braiding Sweetgrass: Indigenous Wisdom, Scientific Knowledge, and the Teachings of Plants*. Milkweed Editions, 2015.

Little Bear, L. "Jagged Worldviews Colliding." *Reclaiming Indigenous Voice and Vision* 77 (2000): 85–108.

Meyer, M. (2001) "Our Own Liberation: Reflections on Hawaiian Epistemology." *The Contemporary Pacific*, 13, no. 1 (2001): 124–148.

Mohawk, J. "Animal Nations and Their Right to Survive." *Daybreak Magazine*, Summer 1988.

Nelson, M. K. *Original Instructions: Indigenous Teachings for a Sustainable Future*. New York: Simon and Schuster, 2008.

Nelson, M. K., and D Shilling. Traditional Ecological Knowledge: Learning from Indigenous Practices for Environmental

Sustainability. Cambridge, UK: Cambridge University Press, 2018.

Sale, K. *The Conquest of Paradise: Christopher Columbus and the Columbian Legacy.* New York: Knopf, 1990.

Watts, A. *Nature, Man and Woman.* New York: Vintage Books, 1991.

Wildcat, D. R. "Vine Deloria, Jr.: Indigenous Iconoclast." In *Neglected Social Theorists of Color: Deconstructing the Margins,* edited by Korey Tillman, David Dickens, and C. C. Herbison. Lanham, MD: Lexington Books, 2023, 29–46.

Wildcat, D. R. (2023) "Traditional Ecological Knowledges: An Antidote to Destruction." In *Re-Indigenizing Ecological Consciousness and the Interconnectedness to Indigenous Identities,* edited by Michelle Montgomery. Lanham, MD: Lexington Books, 1–10.

Wildcat, D. R. (2022) "Earth—A Place for Indigenous Solutions." In *A Companion to Public Philosophy,* edited by Lee McIntyre and Nancy McHugh. New York: Wiley-Blackwell, 95–105.

Wildcat, D. R. *Red Alert! Saving the Planet with Indigenous Knowledge.* Golden, CO: Fulcrum Publishing, 2009.

Other Books in the
Speaker's Corner Series

On Censorship: A Public Librarian Examines Cancel Culture in the US, by James LaRue

———

"A masterful story that illuminates a bold and vivid tapestry of hypocrisy and greed, which drives today's cancel culture." —Nancy Kranich

On Digital Advocacy: Saving the Planet While Preserving Our Humanity, by Katie Boué

———

The guidebook for saving the planet while preserving and protecting your human spirit.

On the Gaze: Dubai and Its New Cosmopolitanisms, by Adrianne Kalfopoulou

———

An immersive experience of Dubai, complete with vivid portraits, elegant prose, and historical context.

About the Cover Art and Artist

About the Cover Art

During the Treaty Times (1850 to 1890) when land was stolen from Native Americans by the US government, many of our chiefs gave important speeches. Amongst one of the most important was Chief Sealth's (Seattle) who spoke passionately about the loss of trees from logging, the pollution from sawmills and industry, and the waning of the natural world. Many environmental writers have repeated his words for more than 150 years. Chief Seattle was Salish (Duwamish and Suquamish), a language that was part of my linguistic group. I see him as a visionary and an important speaker who had great wisdom.

About the Artist

 Jaune Quick-to-See Smith calls herself a cultural arts worker. She uses humor and satire to examine myths, stereotypes, and the paradox of American Indian life in contrast to

the consumerism of American society. Her work is philosophically centered by her strong traditional beliefs and political activism. Smith is internationally known as an artist, curator, lecturer, printmaker, and freelance professor as well as a mentor, for she believes that Giving Back is a life philosophy. She was born at St. Ignatius Mission, raised by her father who was an illiterate horse trader, had her social security card at age eight when she started work as a field hand year-round, and she worked as a waitress and in the canneries throughout high school. Smith earned an art education degree at Framingham State in Massachusetts (now University) and a master's in art at the University of New Mexico. Before completing her degree, Smith began exhibiting in New York at the Kornblee Gallery and organizing Native exhibitions. She has organized and curated more than thirty Native exhibitions in forty-plus years.

Smith has given more than 200 lectures at museums and universities internationally and has shown in over 125 solo exhibits and over 650 group exhibits. Her work is in collections such as Victoria and Albert Museum, London; the Brooklyn Museum; the Museum of Modern Art, Quito, Ecuador; the Whitney Museum, New York; the Walker, Berlin Museum of Ethnology, Germany; the University of Regina, Canada; and the Museum of Modern Art in New York. Smith holds five honorary degrees and numerous awards such as the 1987 Academy of Art and Letters, Purchase Award, New York; 1995 Painting Award, Fourth International Bienal,

Cuenca, Ecuador; 1996 Joan Mitchell Foundation Award; 1997 Women's Caucus for Art, Lifetime Achievement; 2005 New Mexico Governor's Award; 2011 induction into the National Academy of Design; 2012 Georgia O'Keeffe Museum, Living Artist of Distinction; Honorary BA Degree, Salish Kootenai College, Montana; 2018 Montana Governor's Award; 2018 Lifetime Achievement Award in Printmaking, Southern Graphics Council International; 2019 Murray Reich Award, New York; 2020 United States Artists Fellowship; 2021 Brazilian Biennial; 2022 Barnard Medal of Distinction, Anonymous Was a Woman Award; and the 2023 Archives of American Art Medal.

About the Author

Photo by Meredith Mashburn

Daniel R. Wildcat is a Yuchi member of the Muscogee Nation of Oklahoma. Dr. Wildcat received an interdisciplinary PhD from the University of Missouri at Kansas City, and his service as teacher and administrator at Haskell Indian Nations University spans thirty-seven years. He was the Gordon Russell visiting professor of Native American Studies at Dartmouth College in 2013. In 1994, he partnered with the Hazardous Substance Research Center at Kansas State University to create the Haskell Environmental Research Studies (HERS) Center and subsequently start the HERS summer undergraduate internship program with KU professor Dr. Joane Nagel. He is a noted speaker on Traditional Ecological Knowledges and has offered programs for the National Oceanic and Atmospheric Administration, NASA, the American Geophysical Union, the Ecological Society of America, the University Corporation for Atmospheric Research, and many scientific organizations and universities.

Dr. Wildcat is currently the principal investigator of a 20-million-dollar, five-year, NSF-funded project to develop the Rising Voices, Changing Coasts Research Hub at Haskell: a research hub where Indigenous knowledges will be intrinsic to climate science developed to understand climate change impacts on Indigenous coastal Peoples of the US and its territories. He is the author and editor of several books: *Power and Place: Indian Education in America*, with Vine Deloria, Jr.; *Destroying Dogma: Vine Deloria's Legacy on Intellectual America*, with Steve Pavlik; and *Red Alert! Saving the Planet with Indigenous Knowledge. On Indigenuity: Learning the Lessons of Mother Earth* explores Indigenous ingenuity— Indigenuity—and shares examples of its power in addressing the environmental crises of the Anthropocene. In addition, he is a co-author of the Southern Great Plains chapter of the Fourth National Climate Assessment.